GREAT WAR LITERATURE

NOTES

Written by W Lawrance

on

EDWARD THOMAS

SELECTED POEMS

Great War Literature Notes on Edward Thomas, Selected Poems
Written by W Lawrance

Published by:
Great War Literature Publishing LLP
Forum House, Stirling Road, Chichester PO19 7DN
Web site: www.greatwarliterature.co.uk
E-Mail: enquiries@greatwarliterature.co.uk

Produced in Great Britain

ISBN 978-1905378340 (1905378343) Paperback Edition

10 9 8 7 6 5 4 3 2 1

Design and production by Great War Literature Publishing LLP
Typeset in Neue Helvetica, ITC Berkeley Old Style and Trajan Pro

CONTENTS
(arranged chronologically)

(

PREFACE

Great War Literature Publishing provides analysis of literature written about the First World War, whether modern or contemporary. In the case of Edward Thomas, it is a matter of conjecture as to whether his works can be seen as war poetry, or not and for the most part, their subject matter, with a few exceptions, is nature and the countryside. However, all of the poems contained in these study notes were written during the First World War and have come to be perceived as relating to that conflict, so we have chosen to provide notes for those which are most widely studied.

BIOGRAPHY OF EDWARD THOMAS

Born in London on 3rd March 1878, Philip Edward Thomas was the oldest of six sons. His parents (Philip Henry Thomas and Mary Elizabeth Townsend), although originally from Wales, classified themselves as Londoners. Edward grew up in various parts of London, including Lambeth, Wandsworth, Clapham and Balham, but due to frequent holidays spent in Wales and Wiltshire, he soon developed a life-long interest in nature and the countryside.

These holidays were special to Edward set in his favourite countryside and often spent with his mother, at the homes of relatives, including his grandmother, whose cooking he particularly enjoyed. The relationship between mother and son was strong, unlike that between Edward and his father (a civil servant), which was strained and difficult and would remain so. Edward, like many boys of his time, could be sadistic in his childhood games, especially towards other children and animals, although he did keep pigeons. He admitted that he did not make friends easily, with the exception of a couple of other boys, but that he found girls attractive and easy to attract from an early age.

Edward attended various Board, Independent and Grammar schools before being enrolled at St Paul's in Hammersmith at the age of fifteen. In many ways, he was a typical Edwardian schoolboy who, by today's standards, could appear harsh. His image, during his schooldays, was that of a loner. When he attended the Board school, he felt himself to be superior to his fellow students, but found the tables turned when he enrolled at the independent schools, and - especially - at St Paul's, where the children came from families with a great deal more money than his own.

By 1894, Edward had begun writing essays and turned to editor and essayist James Ashcroft Noble, who encouraged his writing and urged him to send his essays to the weeklies for publication. During his meetings with Noble, Edward met his daughter, Helen, a year his senior, who was instantly attracted to the tall, blond, handsome writer. Her father encouraged this friendship, but her mother was less keen and when James Ashcroft Noble died two years later, Helen's mother banned the two from meeting again. This move forced Helen to leave home, taking up the position of a nursery governess, in order to continue her relationship with Edward. Within the year, Edward had taken up a place at Lincoln College, Oxford and he and Helen had become lovers.

He embarked keenly on university life, becoming an avid rower, while still enjoying long walks in the countryside, which had always been, and would remain, a constant feature of his life. He returned home to Helen during the Easter holidays on 1899 and it was at this time that their first child was conceived. Once Helen's pregnancy became known to the couple, they decided to marry, and did so in a small, secretive service on 20th June 1899 at Fulham Registry Office. This event caused a final, irreparable rift between Helen and her mother. Edward and Helen's only son, Philip Merfyn, was born on 15th January 1900.

Edward Thomas graduated from Oxford later that year, but with the pressure of a young family to feed and house, he failed to achieve the high honours that would be required to ensure an academic career. His father tried to push him towards jobs in the civil service or teaching - not what Thomas wanted, but well-paid enough to provide a secure income for his young family. Thomas angrily declined all offers of assistance and prohibited his father from interfering any further in his career.

Thomas was determined to make his way by writing, no matter how difficult the road might be and the young family lived initially in London. However, Thomas was drawn to the countryside and in 1901 they moved to Bearsted near Maidstone in Kent, where a year later, their first daughter, Rachel Mary Bronwen, was born. Thomas's choice of career had resulted in the family living in difficult financial circumstances until he gained a commission, writing a book about Oxford: a job which came with a £100 advance, as well as work writing book reviews for daily newspapers. This type of work was not, however, what Thomas had envisaged as his literary career: instead of creating masterpieces, he was forced to become a "hack", in his own words, adding to his sense of frustration.

By this time, Thomas had begun to spend less and less time at home, finding Helen's company almost intolerable and disliking the domesticity of the household environment. A vicious cycle ensued, whereby the children and Helen would drive Thomas to say and do hurtful things toward them, which would, in turn, make him feel angry and resentful - as well as guilty - although he would blame them for the situation having begun in the first place. In order to work in peace, he rented a study for himself which was a mile away from the family home and communicated with Helen mainly by letter, while he was there.

Edward, Helen and their two young children moved house several times before settling at Steep, near Petersfield in Hampshire at the end of 1906 and again, Thomas set up a separate study, away from the family residence. By now he was earning around £250 per annum, which compared favourably with a schoolmaster, and was approximately five times the income of a farmworker. Despite their improved finances, Thomas remained dissatisfied, commenting to friends that he would prefer to live alone. Helen taught in the Kindergarten at nearby Bedales School, which was also attended by both children. In August 1910, a second daughter, Helen Elizabeth Myfanwy, was born, thus completing Edward's family, although he was, as ever, absent from home when she was born. All three children were known by the Welsh names, rather than their English ones.

In spite of her husband's frequent absences from home - some of which could last for months on end, Helen's love remained constant. She even blamed herself for the situation, wishing that she could do more to help Edward, and believing that he was really rather ashamed of her lack of conventional beauty and intelligence.

The depression, which had first begun to plague him at university, was now becoming predominant in his life and he made at least one very half hearted suicide attempt. Thomas consulted with doctors and psychologists (a new profession at the time in England) and, eventually found solace in Godwin Baynes, a psychoanalyst whom Thomas first consulted in April 1912. Baynes encouraged Thomas to look to himself for happiness, rather than relying on others.

In November 1912, Edward met Eleanor Farjeon who became a close friend and frequent visitor to the Thomas family home, as well as a valued critic of his poetry. She also undertook the task of typing out his manuscripts and sending them off to publishers, all of whom rejected them. Eleanor was in love with Edward, but she never revealed this to him, since she feared that such a declaration would end their friendship. Eleanor did, however, confess her feelings for Edward, to Helen offering to sever all ties with the family. Rather than banishing Eleanor from the house and their relationship, Helen took the unusual step of actively including her rival in family affairs, concluding (quite rightly) that as long as Edward remained oblivious to the situation and faithful to her, everything would be alright.

In the meantime, Edward was not oblivious to the attentions of other women, who found him attractive. He is not known to have been actively unfaithful to Helen, but he certainly enjoyed the company of other women at various times during their marriage.

Professionally speaking, the greatest influence in Edward's life came in 1913, when he was first introduced to the American poet, Robert Frost. He and his family were frequent visitors to the Thomas household and the two writers became firm friends, with Thomas writing positive reviews of Frost's poetry and enhancing the American's poetic career. In return, Frost actively encouraged Thomas to write poetry, especially based on his prose nature writings, which is how his early poems developed in December 1914.

Thomas was an avid reviewer of poetry, helping to make the names of many young poets at the time, including Rupert Brooke and Wilfrid Wilson Gibson and many others. He and Frost also formed part of the "Dymock" group of poets, although at the time, Thomas was the only member who was not actively writing poetry.

When war was declared in August 1914, Thomas was under no obligation to enlist, since he was too old. He considered many options, including returning to America with the Frosts to enhance his fledgling poetic career, before deciding to enlist in the Artists Rifles in July 1915. Eleanor Farjeon noted, at this time, that, having made this decision, he seemed greatly relieved and less tormented than she had ever known him. He had come to believe, quite literally, that he was fighting for the very essence of England.

Thomas spent several weeks as a map-reading instructor at Hare Hall Camp, in Essex. He could have remained safely in England but, again began, again, to wrestle with his conscience as to whether he should do more. In the autumn of 1916, Thomas made his choice and applied for a commission in the Royal Garrison Artillery. He embarked for France, with 244 Siege Battery, as a Second Lieutenant, on the 29th January 1917, by which time all of his 144 poems had already been written, the first few under the name of Edward Eastaway to separate them from his reviews and critical writings - Eastaway being his paternal grandfather's middle name. Thomas had said his final goodbyes to Helen on 11th January: he practical, dealing with finances; she desolate and wondering how she would cope without him. During his time at the Front, he wrote regular letters home to Eleanor and Helen who lived in the hope of him returning safely, as he had promised he would.

On Easter Sunday 1917, Thomas wrote a happy letter to Helen, in which he described the joyous sounds of hedge sparrows, which he had managed to discern in between the noise of the shellfire and guns. In the same post as this letter, Helen received news from one of Edward's brother officers, giving her details of the event she had long dreaded: Edwards death from a shell-blast on Easter Monday, 9th April 1917.

Helen was, understandably, devastated to receive news of Edward's death, as was Eleanor Farjeon who at Helen's request stayed with the young widow and her children for a few weeks, helping where she could with household duties and in looking after the children. Eleanor was deeply affected by the sight of Helen's grief and this made her appreciate, more than ever, that the war was shattering, irrevocably, the lives of so many people.

Edward Thomas is buried at Agny Military Cemetery, in the Pas de Calais, France. His name is one among fifteen other war poets, engraved on a large commemorative stone in Poet's Corner in Westminster Abbey.

Critical acclaim for Edward Thomas's work was slow in coming, despite Helen's efforts to bring it to the public's attention following his death. Over more recent years, however, his poetry has come to be regarded as an honest and sincere reflection of a poet and his time, his beloved countryside and a way of life which would soon be lost forever..

EDWARD THOMAS
Analysis of Selected Poems

March

(Written 5th December 1914)

INTRODUCTION

March is one of the poems which has been included in the OCR A-Level selection, in which it is difficult to perceive a First World War connection, even though the examining board and, therefore, many teachers and students would appear to believe that there must be one. Thomas is now perceived (rightly or wrongly) as a war poet, but this does not mean that all of his poetry is "war poetry", and he certainly never wrote about the trenches or the immediate effects of war and wrote no poetry at all once he had embarked for France. I have, however, been asked to include these less obvious poems in this collection of analysis, despite my misgivings as to their suitability to fit into the genre of war poetry. Due to these doubts on my part, I have provided two versions of my analysis: one relates to the poem as I believe it was intended - a nature piece, based on Thomas's early prose writings; the second provides some First World War links, although it must be noted that these are very loose, obscure and hard to find. Nonetheless, I have provided them, because I have been requested to treat the poem as a war poetry. Whether or not each reader chooses to do likewise is entirely up to them.

BACKGROUND

This poem was written in December 1914, and was Edward Thomas's third poem. These early pieces were almost entirely based around Thomas's prose writings, as he had been advised by his friend, the American poet, Robert Frost, that his travel and nature writing, composed during the previous few years, was actually a good basis for a first foray into serious poetry composition. At around this time, in early January 1915, Thomas had severely sprained his ankle and was confined to the family home at Number Two, Yew Tree Cottages, Church Road at Steep, in Hampshire, where he settled down to write poetry seriously for the first time. His manuscripts were typed out by his friend and fellow poet, Eleanor Farjeon and were often despatched to Frost for comment and approval. Thomas was also in the process of wondering what he ought to do with regard to the war and enlisting. He was really under no obligation to volunteer, due to his age, but felt a sense of love and duty towards his country that caused him some degree of heartache when compared to his feelings of love and responsibility towards his family. Thomas was contemplating taking his wife and three children to America with the Frosts, who were due to return to their homeland at the end of January. As it was, Thomas decided against this and only his oldest child, Mervyn travelled to the United States. Edward Thomas eventually decided to enlist in July 1915, joining the Artist's Rifles. We can, therefore, see that at the time of writing March, Thomas was probably preoccupied by his own indecision over the war, coupled with his uncertainty over his future as a poet and was also possibly house-bound and frustrated.

The precise basis for this poem, however, can be traced to a prose book that Thomas had written entitled *In Pursuit of Spring*, which had been published in April 1914. Here, he tells the story of his bicycle journey between London and the Quantock Hills in Somerset during the spring of 1913. At the beginning of the book he recalls planning his trip in a cold, damp February London, when the grey, unwelcoming skies had made him long for the more familiar countryside and the coming of spring. This planning took Thomas a month, as he had decided to depart on Good Friday (March 21st), so as to travel in warmer weather, with the advantage of the anticipated arrival of spring, to make his journey more appealing. The book ends on an optimistic note, since Thomas feels he has discovered spring in the Quantocks: the budding flowers and trees, as well as the young chirping birds offer him a hope for the future which had, at times during his journey, seemed wanting. Nonetheless, he realises that, for spring to arrive and flourish, winter must perish and die, which in turn, seems to make him a little reflective and sad. Upon reading this account, Robert Frost earnestly urged Thomas to write poetry based upon his journey; his words already being so lyrical and descriptive, needed only to take the poetic form.

MARCH AS A NATURE POEM

Although we know that this poem was definitely not written in the month of March, that is the title Thomas has given to the piece, presumably because that is when he made his journey "in pursuit of spring". The title could have a secondary meaning, however, representing the relentless "march" of time, as one season follows another.

The poem opens with the positive statement, echoed from the end of Thomas's prose account, in which he feels certain that spring will soon be upon him again. This is not only a literal statement, reflecting the changing seasons, but also suggests a favourable attitude in general, whether talking about the weather, or the regrowth of plants and animals.

Next, Thomas refers to the "cold burning" of his skin - an oxymoron which perfectly describes the sensation one receives when coming into the warm, having been outside in the cold air. Thomas goes on to explain that he has been exposed to "hail and wind", which have caused the discomfort to his skin, as well as an aching to his temples. He describes how the tender, young primroses have been damaged by this weather and yet they have survived and are being dried out and brought back to life by the "mighty sun".

However, this initial optimism is soon dashed, as Thomas evidently believes the sunshine (possibly representing his hope for the future and the coming of spring) has actually come too late for the dying flowers. The cold winter has proved too much for them: the weight of the wet, damp weather has been overwhelming and Thomas explains that the spring - or hope of it - has become "lost" among the irrepressible darkness of the winter. This signifies a sense of hopelessness, despite his attempts to point out his assurance that he knows the spring will eventually reappear, nature is doing her utmost to thwart any underlying optimism. The "mountains chill", in which the spring seems to have lost itself, probably represent the clouds, which Thomas had described in his prose account as "white mountains, massive and almost motionless, in the south above the Downs".

Thomas then moves on to describe the birdsong, which is actually absent, kept at bay by the "rain, snow, sleet, hail", although in an hour of respite, the birds manage to sing for a while. During this brief interlude, however, they also have to pack in all their other activities, among which Thomas includes fighting. Their song, during this time, appears to Thomas to be "sweet" since, having not sung for so long, their singing appears almost musical.

In the strange clarity of night, Thomas becomes aware of the "silence" that surrounds him, even though it is still "stained" with the birdsong. This staining suggests damage, but not a sense of permanence, as though the spring will eventually be able to conquer any harm caused by the harsh winter. The noise - or possibly the lack of it - tells him that spring will definitely return, perhaps sooner than he had hoped.

There seems little doubt, having read Thomas's prose account of his journey, and his search for spring that this poem reflects the poet's uncertainty as to whether the harsh winter might have ruined the forthcoming, more fruitful season, beyond repair. As a follower of nature and the countryside, Thomas knows that this cannot really be the case, hence his occasional bursts of optimism. Yet, he also appears somewhat tired and uncertain about the forthcoming spring, wondering perhaps if it will bring forth everything which his journey has led him to anticipate, or whether he will remain disappointed and cold for a little longer still.

MARCH AS A WAR POEM

From a war poetry perspective, the title of the poem could be interpreted as a reference to the marching of men off to war, which could, in turn, be seen as bringing about an inevitable ending, just like "the grave of winter" to quote from the title of the final chapter of Thomas's prose book.

The opening of the poem may also have loose First World War connections, in that many poets began to see the war as a dark, winter-like shadow, where peace would become representative of spring and new beginnings. In this opening, therefore, it is possible that Thomas is commenting upon his certainty that spring will arrive literally as well as metaphorically, since he may have hoped - like many - that the war, still in its early stages at the time this poem was written, would not last for every much longer.

Thomas's description of the half-battered primroses could be seen as a metaphor for the soldiers, who have been "torn" by a "hail" of bullets and shells. In Thomas's initially idealised version of events, these men will rise up again, made strong by the "mighty sun" and move on to better things. However, it soon becomes clear that Thomas's initial optimism is ill-founded. Men cannot be brought back from the dead; the war has killed them off and no amount of hope for the future will bring them back.

The poet's allusions to birdsong being heard in brief moments of silence are quite reminiscent of the accounts of many soldiers, who give reports of hearing birds singing in the interludes of quiet in between bombardments. Additionally, Thomas's references to "rain, snow, sleet, hail" could also be taken as metaphors for the continuous bombardment of artillery, as well as the relentless bad weather.

The "silence" that surrounds the poet may be an allusion to the comparative peace that exists on the battlefields (due to the fact that it is winter and much less fighting is taking place). This, coupled with the interruptions of the birdsong, give him reason to hope for a more lasting peace in the future.

CONCLUSION

The timing of the writing of this poem is quite significant, as we know it was written in December 1914. During this time, there was relatively little activity on the Western Front, with only two minor battles taking place at Givenchy and Champagne in December. These followed, however, on the heels of the First Battle of Ypres, which had been a very costly attack, lasting for over a month, culminating on 22nd November. Thus the stalemate that ensued until the following spring, broken by the Battle of Neuve-Chapelle in March, could be seen as a silence falling over the Western Front. The hope that peace might follow was, of course, futile, but this feeling was not unusual among poets, especially the non-combatants, who did not appreciate that, despite the evident appearance of silence and inactivity, the war was still going on. Others among the war poets who covered this topic - albeit more directly and obviously - included Edith Nesbit, Charlotte Mew, Vera Brittain, Agnes Grozier Herbertson and Sara Teasdale, all of whom focused on the question of whether spring would ever be able to reappear, given the terrible horrors and losses of the war. They simply could not equate the deaths on the battlefields with the idea of hope for the future and rebirth, which is normally associated with spring. Their ideals differ from those of Edward Thomas, at least in part, because of the date at which they wrote their poems. While *March* is an extremely early piece, the other poets mentioned above were writing much later in the war, when there was no longer the same degree of hope that the fighting would soon be over. Also, some of the other poets, such as Vera Brittain, had been personally affected by the war, having lost loved-ones, so it was more difficult for them to think positively about the future.

As a poem written early in Thomas's poetic career, this piece shows great promise of the talents that were to follow in his more obvious war poetry, as Thomas displays his lyrical abilities, as well as his observational and language skills, which he had honed in the writing of prose. For example, his description of the birds singing as "… they cared not what they sang or screamed, / Whether 'twas hoarse or sweet or fierce or soft," is accurate both of birdsong and a bombardment, if one allows the guns to have a personality, as many poets did. However, lines such as this mainly show the effect which the continuous noise of the birds singing might have on one listening: it is pleasurable for a while, "and after", but can also feel like a cacophony of relentless screaming. Thomas's observation of these points, and the reader's ability to impose a war-time meaning onto them, are what makes his poetry so unusual.

OLD MAN

(Written 6th December 1914)

Old Man is one of the poems included in the OCR A-Level selection in which I find it difficult to perceive any real First World War connections. The purpose of Great War Literature Publishing is to write about and analyse the literature of and about the First World War and, as such, I would ordinarily exclude poems such as this. However, I have been requested to include an analysis of all fifteen poems within the OCR selection, which (rightly or wrongly) seem to be perceived as war poetry, and their author as a war poet. In the case of Old Man, there is only a vague and very loose connection to the war, which I have detailed and otherwise, in my opinion, it remains an early Thomas poem of nature and memory.

Written in early December 1914, *Old Man* was Edward Thomas's fourth poem. This piece was first written as a prose account entitled Old Man's Beard, in which the language and some of the phrases can be seen to be almost identical to those employed in the poem. Thomas had written the prose piece a couple of weeks before composing the poem and it tells of "the baby" (his youngest daughter Myfanwy) picking at the leaves of the bush known as "old man's beard". Thomas goes on to recount his daughter's reaction to the smell of the plant and then to his own memories. A great deal of the terminology is exactly the same, when one studies the two pieces and it would seem that Thomas was writing the account in prose first, as a medium with which he felt more accustomed and more comfortable, before converting his words into a poetic form.

The title of the poem relates in the first instance to the plant named Southernwood, which is also known as "Old Man" or "Lad's Love", amongst other nicknames. This is a flowering plant, which has a camphor-like smell (making it reminiscent of mothballs and somewhat unpleasant), and has small feathery leaves and yellow flowers. The plant has antiseptic qualities, being used to treat disorders of the liver and spleen, as well as stomach ailments. Romans believed it protected men from impotence and Mediterranean men would rub in to their chins to promote beard growth. The Latin name for the plant is Artemisia Abrotanum, after the goddess Artemis, who represents hunting, wild animals, wilderness, virginity and childbirth. As such, the poem's title may simply be a representation of this plant and its associations. However, it is interesting to note that Thomas doesn't refer to the poem by any of the plant's other names such as "Lover's Plant", "Garderobe", or "Maid's Ruin". Instead, he chooses "Old Man", which may be a reflection of how he felt about himself. Thomas was thirty six years old when he wrote this poem, but may have been feeling old beyond his years at a time when his own children were growing up and also many younger men were volunteering to go to war.

As the poem opens, it becomes clear that Thomas is suffering from a sense of confusion or loss. He points out that he is caught between youth and old age, which makes his recollection of this plant quite appropriate, given that two of its names represent both of these stages of life. He goes on to accurately describe the leaves of the plant as being "hoar-green" and "feathery", the former being an oxymoron, since "hoar" means greyish-white. Nonetheless, his description is sound, since the leaves of the plant are greyish-green with white tinges and they do resemble "feathery" fronds. The plant, he says, has many names, which contradict and confound, but which fail to really explain the purpose of the bush. However, the plant doesn't really need all these names in order to be itself. Nonetheless, Thomas likes them, perhaps because the names give the plant a sense of history and personality.

While Thomas claims to appreciate the names, he doesn't feel so generously towards the actual plant itself. This may be because of the unpleasant scent it gives off. The only saving grace is associations with the plant, which cause him to "love it". Thomas refers now to a "child", which - as with the prose account, would have meant his daughter Myfanwy, as she was invariably the subject of his poems in which he alludes to an unnamed young child (as in Snow or The Brook). Here, Thomas explains that the child's reaction to the plant is to play with its leaves; to crush and snip at them and then drop them onto the ground, effectively killing them. She doesn't like the smell: one sniff at her fingers and she leaves the plant alone, running off to find something else to do. While playing with the plant, however, it is as though the child becomes quite thoughtless as to the damage she is inflicting. Thomas notes that the child's continuous picking at the plant has stunted its growth, meaning that once something has been damaged in this way, the damage is permanent and long-lasting, possibly affecting future generations, who won't be able to enjoy the plant to its fullest potential. His implication, as a lover of the countryside and ecologist, could also be that the child thrives at the expense of the plant.

Next, Thomas wonders - perhaps because of the child's silence - whether she will remember the garden in the future, or whether the unpleasant scent of the plant will deter her memories of more pleasant things, among which he includes not only other plants, but also himself, as he forbids her to continue picking at the leaves of the bush, presumably because he fears that, by her actions, she may be causing it too much harm.

Thomas states that he cannot remember where he first smelled the scent of the plant and, in order to recapture the memory, he sometimes picks the leaves and sniffs at them himself, to try to bring the memories back to life, although this doesn't work. Despite his distaste for the scent of the plant, Thomas says he would rather have this than the smell of sweeter things, because this holds more memories for him. However, in spite of all his efforts, Thomas can't actually recall the precise memories that haunt him. He's lost "the key", or the trigger that would provoke the memory and bring back the thought of when he first came across the smell. In fact, the scent, which he hopes will recapture the memories, actually seems to make his mind go blank: perhaps his senses are overpowered by the strength of the smell, so he cannot function sensually as he normally would.

As Thomas smells at the plant, he is struck by his remarkable lack of memories: there is no garden, or path; the bush itself cannot be recalled any longer. He remarks on the absence of the child and parents, although whether the child is Myfanwy or a memory of himself, and the parents are his own, or refer to himself and his wife Helen, is not so clear. He could, at this stage, be trying to recall distant memories of his own childhood, rather than those relating to his daughter. There is a sense of loneliness here which seems to tie in with Thomas's own upbringing, as he was quite a loner as a child.

Thomas goes on to state that he can only clearly see an "avenue" - a road to the future, rather than the past, perhaps - except that this is not hopeful, but rather forbidding, since it is "dark" and "nameless", with no end in sight. This last reference is the only real possible First World War connection, in that Thomas appears to be using his lack of memories to look forward, although to an equally non-existent future. He associated enlistment and overseas service with the certainty of death, ensuring that his past and his future would - in his own mind - become irrelevant.

This is rather a sad poem, in which the poet appears somewhat lost, trapped between youth and old age, in an effective mental and emotional no man's land. The loss of his detailed memories seems to trouble him, as he projects these thoughts onto his future, for which he has no hopes or prospects. It also seems that he may be examining the question of whether unpleasant memories of the past banish any pleasant memories that might have existed. It appears that, no matter how hard he tries, his memories have disappeared and that the unattractive smell of the plant is his excuse, or "key" as to why this might have happened.

Another of Thomas's poems, which has a similar tone is *Melancholy*, in which he expresses his resignation and surrender towards his own sense of sadness and inability to make a decision, up to the point where this becomes overwhelming, dominating his life, as does his search for his memories in *Old Man*. These two poems demonstrate the compulsive elements of Thomas's nature, as well as his depressive personality, and show how he was capable of focusing on one aspect of his life exclusively and, some might say, quite selfishly.

A PRIVATE

(Written 6th-7th January 1915)

The title of this poem is interesting since it gives the nameless subject anonymity - he could be any one of the thousands of dead privates currently lying in unknown graves in France.

The subject being a ploughman is representative of Thomas's beloved countryside - a common theme in his poetry which is repeated in the later poem As the Team's Head-Brass. We are informed very early in this poem that the soldier is dead, which, together with the representation of frosty nights gives the beginning of the poem a cold and almost depressing edge. Then we learn that, in life this man was merry which contrasts with the earlier impression and causes great feelings of regret that one so happy should now be dead.

Whilst at home in England, the ploughman had often slept out of doors, despite the cold and when asked by anyone where he slept, would respond that he slept in a specific hawthorn bush. Interestingly, the bush is given a proper name, while the ploughman is not, showing that to Thomas, the countryside is as important (if not more so) as the people who reside in it. Nobody ever knew where this bush was, implying that the man may have invented this place, so as to keep his real hideaway a secret. In fact, we learn, the downs above the town are filled with many such bushes, any one of which might be hiding a sleeping countryman. Thomas tells us the name of the pub in which the ploughman used to drink, thus removing some of his anonymity, giving him a more human quality and, therefore, forcing us to care even more about his death. We are finally reminded that this serene image of country life is now spoiled because the ploughman went to war, became a private and gave his life. He lies somewhere in France, but, as in life, his exact whereabouts are a secret. Like many of the dead, he - as yet - has no known grave.

This poem was written early in 1915, possibly while Thomas was recovering from a severely sprained ankle, and regretting his missed opportunity to travel to America with Robert Frost. He was, at this stage, still undecided as to whether or not to enter the war.

Unlike many of Thomas's other poems, this is not overtly patriotic, and although he creates an idyllic scene of the Wiltshire countryside, he makes no mention of preserving England and her ways and beauty. Instead, this poem is more a celebration of the simple country folk who have gone to war and will not return. His love for the countryside still shines through as he praises the honesty, serenity and courage of these men who have, without great clamour or fuss, given everything for their country.

TEARS

(Written 8th January 1915)

This poem was written in January 1915, before Edward Thomas enlisted, and at this point in time, he had a severely sprained ankle and was confined to home. He occupied his time writing poetry, which was typed up for him by fellow poet, Eleanor Farjeon, whom he had met in November 1912. The two had immediately formed a close friendship which, for Eleanor soon blossomed into love, although she always remained silent upon the subject, fearing that, if she revealed her true feelings to Edward Thomas, he - as a married man - would feel duty bound to terminate their friendship. She often visited the family home at Steep, near Petersfield in Hampshire and, as Thomas was at this time a virtual invalid, they spent much of the next three months together. It was during this time of quiet inactivity that Thomas really began to contemplate his future. He had, essentially, two options: he could go to America with his friend, Robert Frost and his family, who were due to return there the following month; or he could enlist. As it transpired, only Thomas's 15 year old son, Merfyn travelled to the USA with the Frosts, returning in December; Thomas himself chose the latter option and enlisted in the Artist's Rifles in July.

This was not a straightforward decision, as it might have been for many eager young men in the early days of the war. For a start, Thomas was not really a young man: he was thirty-seven years old when he joined up. Secondly, he had the responsibility of a wife and three children, who depended upon him financially. Finally, he had only just discovered his true poetic strength: encouraged by Robert Frost, he had taken up writing poetry, rather than prose, as recently as December 1914. He must has been asking himself whether he was really prepared to sacrifice all of this. On the other hand, his love for his country and his loyalty towards it, seems to have outweighed all other considerations.

When he finally reached his difficult decision, Eleanor Farjeon noted that he seemed relieved and less tormented than she had ever known him. He believed that, although it would almost certainly cost his life, he was fighting for the very essence of England, and Englishness.

This poem, however, was written while Thomas was struggling to make his decision, grappling with his conscience over whether to stay in his beloved England, or take his family to the safety of America. The opening phrase of the poem refers to Thomas's lost emotions: his tears have dried up, or been used up, presumably in grief. He goes on to wonder why his tears did not fall sooner - although he recollects that they fell, in fact, as "ghosts", or memories, perhaps - on a day when he had witnessed a company of "hounds" (a metaphor for soldiers) passing by. He describes these men as "not yet combed out", implying that they had been volunteers, not yet trained or in uniform, on their way to camp and still wearing their civilian clothes. The fact that they number "twenty" and that Thomas lived in a fairly small village suggests that this group may well have comprised all the local young men. Although they may look "unequal" in their plain clothes, he believes that their united goal of hunting down the enemy gives them a uniformity, making them as "one". Thomas uses loose metaphors here for the story of St George and the Dragon, portraying the men as both "hounds" on the trail of a "scent" (a very English image") and as knights or saviours, in armour, going off to slay the "dragon". In either event, they are portrayed as protectors of the land.

These men, it would seem, have gone off "towards the sun", which may suggest that they march towards the east, being as the sun rises in the east and England's enemies were situated in that direction. Equally, however, one could infer that they were marching towards the sunset (or the west), signifying a metaphor for the end of their lives. The "Blooming Meadow" to which he refers (although it would hardly be "blooming" in January - so this is a memory), would previously have harvested "hops" for making beer. These are all reminders of the countryside, even though it is winter, and the rural pastimes for which Thomas had a fondness. In addition, we are reminded, obliquely, that the young men are no longer able to tend the hops in the meadow, or to drink the beer produced by its harvest.

Next, Thomas recalls another day - another scene - when he ought to have cried (or maybe did). On this occasion, he had been visiting a "tower", which we may assume had two turrets, since it was "double-shadowed". We could also presume that he visited this tower as a tourist and is remembering the visit fondly, recalling details, such as the "sweet" warmth of the "April morning"; the "silence"; the mighty "charm" of the courtyard, which outweighed anything he had found in the tower itself. He recalls the changing of the guard and the "white tunics" of the young "fair-haired and ruddy" soldiers, as well as the music of the "drums and fifes". The cumulative effect of the sounds and scenes had been to drown out the "silence" and "solitude" which formed his normal state of mind. In addition, the recollection of this scene makes him remember things which he had not even considered, but that he has now forgotten - hence his feelings of sorrow. This makes more sense if we remember that this poem was written in January 1915, so the "April morning" of which Thomas is writing must, necessarily, have been before the war. Therefore the soldiers in "white tunics" would be the regulars, who might well have been despatched to France with the original BEF in August 1914, only to perish in the early battles, culminating in the First Battle of Ypres. As such, the "truth" which Thomas might well have forgotten is that these men died first, leaving the young "hounds" of volunteers to take their place. It is easy to see that people might, in those early, complacent days, not have remembered that regular soldiers, although professional, were really just young men too... quite a sorry "truth" to forget.

This is a poem of regret, but also there is a hint of gratitude. As an older man, the injustice of dying youth might well have seemed inexorably sad to Thomas. He describes the men as a thing of "beauty", reminding us again of their youth and, indeed, he has focused throughout on the physical appearance of the men, giving the poem a homoerotic quality. That does not imply that Thomas was homosexual - he wasn't - it only means that he appreciated beauty, in all its forms, and felt desolated by its loss.

The poem shows fewer symptoms of depression than many of Thomas's other pieces and, although there is an underlying sadness, this is not introverted. Indeed, he seems to elevate the sacrifices being made by others, without glorifying either them or their loss. He gives them due stature and deference, affording them the mourning he feels they deserve. His sorrow seems unbounded: even the thought of the men passing and the memory of the soldiers at the tower, moves him to tears. We also know that, at the time of writing, Thomas was contemplating enlisting himself, so he is possibly mourning the potential loss of his own future.

Thomas's language in this poem is deliberately sad and emotive. He uses alliteration sparingly, and only with soft "s" sounds, as in "stirring and sweet" or "strange solitude... silence". Indeed, he mentions "solitude" and "silence" twice within the poem. This creates an almost soporific effect, lulling the reader, subconsciously, into a world of ease and gentleness, which is contrasted with the extreme sadness of the poet's tears, which we know he cried to the point of them running dry. Additionally, he provides another contrast, using the oxymoron of a "rage of gladness" to describe the feelings of the young "hounds" marching off. This represents the feelings of high excitement which volunteers felt in the early days of the war, coupled with their fervent desire to do their duty and fight for their country: the latter emotion ringing very true with Thomas himself.

Although it is only a minor point, one of the most interesting phrases, or concepts, raised within this poem is that of tears having "ghosts". This image, within the context of the First World War, brings to mind the idea of phantom tears, or dead tears: in other words, although it is only 1915, people have already, as Thomas states, cried so much, that their tears no longer seem real or true. At the same time, however, there is a contrasting image created that, in the future, these "ghost" tears will return to haunt the mourners, plaguing them when they thought themselves safe from sadness, when they thought all misery was "forgotten" - just as Thomas seems to have done. In this way, the implication could be that the mourning will never be over, because the "ghosts" will always return, even if only in the form of memories, and tears.

BUT THESE THINGS ALSO

(Written 18th March 1915)

This poem is one among several in the OCR A-Level syllabus in which I find it difficult to perceive any First World War connections, despite the fact that the examining board and many teachers would appear to be assuming that Edward Thomas was exclusively a war poet. Being as the purpose of Great War Literature Publishing is to analyse literature relating to the First World War, I would normally not have included this poem, but have received numerous requests to treat the OCR selection as a whole and have, therefore, reluctantly relented. That said, there really are only very indefinite links between this poem and the conflict and it must be pointed out (or repeated) that, while Thomas wrote all of his poetry during the First World War, that does not mean that we may infer that the conflict always formed a part of his subject matter.

The poem was written on March 18th 1915, at which point Thomas was seriously considering his position with regard to the war. His good friend, the American poet Robert Frost, had returned with his family to his homeland in February, taking Thomas's only son, Merfyn. For several months, Thomas contemplated whether or not to pursue the Frosts to America, with or without his wife and two daughters (who he considered leaving behind). In the end, by July, he had decided to enlist and in December, Merfyn returned to England to rejoin his mother and younger sisters. It was, essentially, Thomas's sense of duty towards his country that kept him bound to its shores, typified by the title of a poetry anthology he prepared and edited at the time: This England.

The poem opens with Thomas noting some of the evident similarities between winter, which is just passing and spring, which is just about to begin. The natural connection between the two seasons, which have assumed links and can sometimes seem to merge together, is initially just pointed out in the shade of the grass. Thomas describes this as having been "long-dead" during the winter months, but now he claims, it has become grey and this, he implies, makes it look less alive than it had during the winter. One might question why the grass doesn't yet look green, but as the second verse progresses, it becomes clear that everything - not just the grass - has a rather unnatural hue of whitish-grey, making it all seem rather monotone and dull.

In this second verse, Thomas expands on this lack of colour, recording the minute details of his surroundings, from the shell of a snail, which we may assume is empty and has been dried out and "bleached", losing its glossy sheen, to the "chips" of flint and chalk that lie around, and the birds' droppings that have splashed the ground. Thomas's description of the latter provides an interesting point of contrast, as the "dung" would not normally be described in terms of its purity, but here Thomas is trying to emphasise the lack of colour everywhere.

Thomas then begins to debate how man so easily mistakes many of these "white things" for the early signs of spring, rather than the continuation of winter. He seems to see winter as something that has protected the land, for which the forthcoming season is obliged to give thanks. Additionally, there is a sense here that nature will always get things right and pay her "debts", while mankind will continue to make "mistakes". This could be seen as a loose reference to the First World War, although this is somewhat vague and convoluted, brought about mainly by Thomas's language, mentioning man's "mistakes" and winter's "ruins", which bring the war to mind, even though this metaphor may not have been the poet's intention.

In the final verse, Thomas comments that, even as the North wind continues to blow, the starlings are trying their best to keep up the appearance that Spring is close at hand, by keeping "their spirits up" despite the bad weather. The starling is not a migratory bird, so would have remained "chattering" throughout the winter. Thomas's point, therefore, is that, in spite of the weather, they are trying to look on the brighter side, anticipating the spring. It was March at the time of writing, so Thomas knows that spring should be "here" and yet, at the same time, winter has still "not gone". This final line could be a metaphor for the First World War, implying that, at the time of writing, although spring may have been on the cusp of arriving, signalled in the form of new battles, such as Neuve-Chapelle (begun on 10th March), this did not mean that the end of the war was in sight. This metaphor may not have been what Thomas had in mind and the end of the piece was more probably connected to his thoughts on his next poem, written on the following day (19th March 1915), entitled *The New House*, in which Thomas examines the themes of change, ageing, grief, and how atmosphere affects mood.

As well as definite links to *The New House*, in both style and content, But these things also can additionally be compared to Thomas's earlier poem, *March*, and also his prose account on which that is based, entitled *In Pursuit of Spring*. We sense in both poems, that Thomas places great value on the seasons, with a special focus on spring, representing birth and growth. Whether or not Thomas perceives this season - like other war poets - as being indicative of peace, is not always very clear, but readers should beware of always giving war-time connotations to Thomas's words.

For Thomas, winter seems representative of death, which is understandable but, more unusually, also of preservation. The colours are dull and lifeless, but he acknowledges that the season's coldness has preserved the countryside, ready for the forthcoming spring. Both poems are not exclusively optimistic about the anticipated season, which might seem fairly unusual. Although Thomas continues to pursue the spring, he doesn't necessarily completely welcome the demise of the winter.

IN MEMORIAM (EASTER 1915)

(Written 6th April 1915)

This poem was written on April 6th 1915, just a few months before Edward Thomas decided to enlist in the Artist's Rifles, which he did in July, at the age of 37. Thomas had spent months deliberating over what he should do: he had a wife and three young children, who were dependent upon him; but he also felt a sense of duty and responsibility towards his country. Eventually, he decided to enlist, believing that he was defending the very essence of England and Englishness - not just a way of life, but the actual soil of the nation.

In Memoriam (Easter 1915) reflects Thomas's perception of the ordinary things that either have already been or will be lost, and that can never be recaptured, which perspective typified the experiences of many during the First World War. Originally, this poem had no title and the manuscript bore just the date upon which it was written. The title by which the poem is now known was evidently added by an editor at a later date. Whether this was done posthumously, bearing in mind that Edward Thomas was killed on Easter Monday 1917, is not known, but it would seem an appropriate tribute to the poet.

The poem opens with what appears to be a simple description of a woodland scene. However, Edward Thomas's language is deceptive: the "flowers" are suggestive of beauty, but are also reminiscent of funerals; the fact that they have been "left thick" reminds the reader not only of a graveyard scene, but also of the knowledge that the woodland is untended, since the young men who might have done this job, have gone off to war. These flowers have not grown naturally, but have been "left", which implies something outside of the natural order: they are discarded and, because they are neglected, they will die, which reminds us of the men dying on the battlefields, their bodies lying "thick" upon the ground.

Thomas's use of the word "nightfall" introduces a sombre, melancholy tone of darkness, which contrasts with the floral opening to the poem, making us realise his true meaning. Flowers usually have a natural association with birth or new beginnings, which a poet would normally connect with dawn. However Thomas wants to create the opposite effect, introducing the gloom of "nightfall" to suggest an ending, rather than a beginning of things. The flowers remind Thomas of the men who are "far from home" - both literally and metaphorically, so here we are led to believe that he is speaking of those who are away from home, serving in France or Flanders, as well as those who are dead and are, therefore, even further from home. The mention of Eastertide is noteworthy, as it is a time of great religious significance, being the fifty days between Easter Sunday and Pentecost Sunday. Ordinarily, this would have been a time of celebration, but during an event as catastrophic as the First World War, it is easy to imagine the conventions of religion being tested. This imagery also provides another contrast between the traditional Easter and Pentecostal celebrations, against the mournful sadness associated with the war.

Edward Thomas goes on to remind the reader that the men who are "far from home" will not walk in the woods "with their sweethearts" again; nor will they gather up the flowers that will continue to grow there, because they will not be returning from the war (or, one may possibly infer that, if they do return, such things will have much less significance for them). This idea reinforces Thomas's view that everything, right down to the basic fundamentals of life, was changing; it was for these things that Thomas was going to fight. His use of the word "gathered" for the picking of the flowers, also brings to mind the harvest, which is another rural and religious celebration, as well as the idea of the men gathering the women into their arms, which - because the men will not be returning - will remain forever empty.

Thomas paints a soft, romantic image of rural England in spring, obliquely contrasting this with the reality of the noise, death and destruction of the battles of the First World War, which, following a pause through the winter of 1914-15, had just begun again with the Battle of Neuve-Chapelle in March. As an older man (he was 37 when he wrote this poem), Thomas was probably also struck by the notion that the younger generation would miss out on the simple pleasures of youth and courtship that he and his wife, Helen had enjoyed and that many young women would be left grieving for lost opportunities.

The language employed in this poem, although evidently simple, is also deliberate. So, for example, Thomas has rhymed "wood" with "should"; the first word creating an air of certainty, the second leaving the reader in doubt. The "wood" is a reference to something that will remain steadfast, regardless of the war; the word "should" reminds us of the intransigence of mankind - that his future is less certain. In addition, the phrasing of the last few words of the poem is deliberately awkward. It would be more normal and flowing to say "and will never do again". However, by delaying the word "never" for as long as is grammatically possible, Thomas not only raises the hopes of his reader, only to dash them, but also creates a more jarring tone to the final words, forcing the reader to contemplate his meaning more closely, rather than taking it for granted.

The poem has a tone of sad reflection and mourning, not only for those who have died and for the everyday activities which they enjoyed, but also for a way of life which Thomas felt was threatened by the war and which he believed could not survive the destruction that the war would inevitably bring to England's shores, fields and woods. Although Thomas may not have entitled this poem himself as "In Memoriam", it is most certainly intended as a lament for the men, women and way of life of a generation that did not realise it was about to become lost.

MELANCHOLY

(Written 25th April 1915)

The title of this poem is fairly self-explanatory in one sense: the meaning of the word "melancholy" being a deep and long-lasting sadness. This emotion exemplifies Edward Thomas's depressive moods, which could overwhelm him. At these times, he would often take himself off into the countryside for days at a time, leaving his family with no idea of his whereabouts, or when he would be likely to return. He had suffered from depression for most of his life, but as he grew older, it became worse and more intense. One might, therefore, assume that this poem is about his feelings during one of his spells of "melancholy", but that would be to underestimate the poet's train of thought, and would show a lack of knowledge with regard to his exact situation at the time of writing.

The poem was written on 25th April 1915, according to the original manuscript, at which point Thomas was in the process of trying to decide whether or not to enlist. This was a difficult decision for Thomas, who was thirty-seven years old at the time and, therefore, not under any obligation to volunteer. He also felt a keen responsibility to his family, who depended on him financially. Added to this was the fact that he firmly believed that, if he did enlist and serve overseas, death would inevitably follow. Nonetheless, all of these feelings were outweighed by his enormous sense of duty towards his country, which he regarded as so much more than just a place where he happened to live. Englishness itself represented something of great importance to Thomas, who believed that he could not really call himself a true Englishman, if he was not prepared to die and preserve his country's way of life. As such, after much deliberation, Thomas decided to enlist in July 1915. At the time of writing this poem, however, not only was he wracked with indecision, but he was also - according to a letter written to his friend and fellow poet, Eleanor Farjeon - suffering from a "chill".

This gives, perhaps, greater credibility to this poem, which can at times seem a little disconnected from reality, but which makes more sense if the writer was suffering from a "fever". As a final background fact, it is worth bearing in mind that, on the Western Front, on 22nd April - three days before this poem was written - the Germans had made the first successful use of chlorine gas at the Second Battle of Ypres.

The poem opens with a repetitive description of the weather. Thomas often uses the elements in this way in his poetry, to denote emotion and here the "rain and wind" would seem to designate monotony (hence the repetition), as well as "melancholy". Although it is springtime, we are not led to believe that this is a light April showery interlude, but rather a prolonged downpour, accompanied by heavy, blasting winds, which combine to make the season seem less tangible. This weather, we are told, raves "endlessly", giving it a human, but somewhat manic quality, which is quite unattractive. The "Summer storm", as Thomas describes it, coupled with the "fever", which is almost certainly the result of his chill, and his customary feelings of "melancholy", work a kind of "magic" on him. This changes his perspective, making him "fear" the company of others, far more than he fears "solitude", quite simply because he finds the thought of peoples' interrupting voices both "too sharp" and "too rude".

Overall, in this opening, Thomas creates an atmosphere of tension and self-absorption, which is not really that unusual in his poetry (see his poem Rain, for a good comparison). It seems that it would not matter to Thomas whether the "company" on offer was that of the "dearest" or "wisest" person he knows: in either case, they would be rejected in favour of "solitude". This thought brings home to the reader the poet's rejection of his family and loved ones at those "melancholy" times, when he sought only the solace of his own company and the peace of nature. Thomas appears to be very restless in this section of the poem, not knowing what he really desires: all he knows is that, whatever choice he makes, it will signify nothing. This is almost certainly a reflection of Thomas's attempts to decide whether or not to enlist at this time; his reasoning being that, either way, he was doomed. If he fought, he believed he would certainly die; if he did not join up, then he would have abandoned his beloved country in her moment of need and, living with that knowledge would have been tortuous for him. This was a lose-lose situation, making his decision difficult: in one direction he faced what he believed to be certain death, with only an outside chance of survival, the consequences of which could be financial ruin for his family. On the other side, he was guaranteed safety, but with the knowledge that his love for his country had not been as strong as he had always needed it to be.

Next, however, the tone of the poem changes, as Thomas realises that, despite his "despair", none of his feelings will make any difference. If anything, the tension makes taking the decision seem even sweeter, which is a way of saying that it is actually more difficult. "Sweetness" is not always a desirable or attractive trait and can be used to represent a type of cloying sickliness, especially given that, in this instance, Thomas describes his "sweetness" as "strange".

In the distance, while listening to the rain and pondering his "choice", he also hears the sound of a "cuckoo" calling. This is an archetypal spring bird, although the poet seems surprised to hear it, given the weather. In this instance, the cuckoo's call is a reference to the changing seasons and also to the fact that, whatever decision Thomas reaches, and whether it rains or not, the cuckoo will continue to sing; the seasons will continue to change; nothing will alter in the natural world. His decision means nothing.

Everything then becomes "soft": the nearby "water falling", rather than just being described as "rain", is now more like a musical instrument. Even softer still - far "remote" in fact (so "remote" that they feel like "history" already) - are the "rumours" he has heard of the war and what it might be doing to either his "friends" or his "foes", or even, for that matter, what it might ultimately do to himself. These "rumours" and how they affect others may be an allusion to the recent gas attack on the Western Front, which might well have damaged his "friends" or allies but which Thomas might well have thought of as damaging to those who created such a fearful weapon that went against nature itself.

There is almost an ecstasy of indecision running through this poem: Thomas has a momentous decision to make, made more complicated by his love for his country and the unremitting voices of those (including himself) who were urging him for decide, one way or the other. This is reflected in the changing tone of the poem, where everything that was "sharp" and "rude" becomes "soft" as his thoughts progress. We can sense that this situation would stretch every nerve within him, making it become almost sweetly destructive - a concept which is quite difficult to understand, except for those who have faced a similar crisis. The uncertainty of his situation, coupled with the fact that he was actually unwell at the time, serves to create an intensely taut atmosphere in which we sense his desire to simply escape from everything into the "magic" of the "Summer storm". This causes him to feel a combination of "melancholy" and "despair"; to crave "solitude" and reject those to whom he might normally turn.

Although Thomas never actually mentions the war in this poem, its presence is presumed by default, provided that the reader understands the poet's situation with regard to his choice, and his state of mind at the time of writing. Without this knowledge, *Melancholy* is really just a nature poem. However, knowing that Thomas was struggling - and had been for many months - to decide which route to follow, makes all the difference when analysing this poem.

While we must acknowledge that there are undertones of resignation, selfishness and surrender here, the poet also allows for some mild hope too. So, the cuckoo still calls and the sound of the rain changes from its monotonous raving to a more musical tone. These are admissions that his decision, for all its personal significance, doesn't really matter: that life will go on for everything and everyone else; which is, after all, rather a "melancholy" thought. The realities of the war are also not allowed to intrude into his thoughts, but are referred to as "rumours", since to believe in the horror of them would make his decision even more difficult still.

Although there is a regular rhyme pattern to this poem, the metre is irregular, so there is no rhythm. This is quite intentional, making the reader feel the poet's tension and difficulty, through the unevenness of his words.

The Glory

(Written early May 1915)

The Glory was written very early in May 1915 and reflects some of Thomas's prose and poetic writings on health and happiness. In his book, *The Heart of England*, published in 1906, Thomas had written that he was uncertain that he was capable of feeling complete happiness, even when that emotion was gifted to him. He seems to have believed that he was unworthy of contentment because he understood too it too completely to ever fully enjoy it: he knew it and its flaws and disappointments too well. Another inspiration behind this poem may have been the writings of Richard Jefferies, whom Thomas greatly admired. In 1883, Jefferies had written of nature's power over man in terms of the giving of strength and happiness. Thomas had written a study of the works of Jefferies, published in 1909, so was very familiar with his philosophies, that man should look to himself to find the true beauty behind what nature has to offer. At the time of writing this poem, Thomas was only weeks away from finally making the decision to enlist, having spent many months deliberating over his family responsibilities and wondering whether to pursue his literary career, either in England or America.

The title of the poem reflects the wonder and "the glory" of the scene, which faces the poet on this particular morning: the marvellous expanse of sky; the fields and forests which, though devoid of activity are full of hidden pleasures. The title may also, however, reflect the "glory", or the honour that might be associated with the idea of volunteering to serve one's country. While the idea of such "glory" might seem outdated today, in early 1915, before the Battle of Loos (that September) and, more importantly, the Battle of the Somme (in the summer of 1916), this sentiment would not have been that uncommon.

The opening of the poem is ripe and overflowing with the imagery of a beautiful dawn, in which the poet appears to find unbounded rapture. The virginal "untouched" qualities, coupled with the various birds, offer the poet a sense of newness and wonder, which appear to take his breath away. His assertion that the "dove" makes him look for something which is even "sweeter than love", might seem surprising, until one understands the mentality of the poet, who placed comparatively little importance on the significance of human love. Thomas had been known to tell his wife, Helen, that he was incapable of love, while also pursuing the affections of other women, either in the form of a muse, or simply because he found them physically attractive. This does not mean to say that Thomas was in love with any of the people in his life and seems, rather more, to have enjoyed inspiring, rather than returning love. However, he was perfectly capable of perceiving and appreciating physical and natural beauty, which he placed above many of the other attributes of life. Here, therefore, his implication would seem to be that the "dove" urges him to seek greater beauties; more natural temptations and breathtaking wonders. Thomas's simile, likening the clouds to "new-mown hay" is taken from his memory, since the poem was written in early May, when there would not have been any newly harvested hay for him to look at. Nonetheless, this comparison makes us realise that the clouds must have a yellowish hue, since the hay would also be that colour, rather than white or grey, like a normal cloud, which reinforces the notion that it is dawn or daybreak.

Thomas then alludes to the enormity of his surroundings; the vast expanse of sky above him; the fields and forests at his feet, all of which are empty and devoid of human interference, although the "heat" causes a haze, which we may assume gives the impression of movement. In reality, however, this signifies nothing and that reflects the hollowness of the poet's "own heart", once again giving the impression that he finds emotional commitment quite difficult.

The poet speaks of how he senses that the wonder of these beautiful surroundings are tempting him to a feeling of fulfilment and satisfaction with which he feels unable to comply. Thomas feels inadequate, it would seem, in the face of such delights, believing that nothing he can ever do or be will be good enough to compare with the sights before him. Their simple colours and movements are more complete and satisfactory than him, making him feel unfit to even be in their presence. This sense of inadequacy is not unusual among those with a depressive nature, such as Thomas's, making one feel that nothing one says or does is quite right or satisfactory. Additionally, however, this passage may signify Thomas's sense of overwhelming passion for his country - outweighing any feelings he has for anything else, including himself, and for which he would ultimately sacrifice his life. At the time of writing, Thomas was only a few weeks away from enlisting, so such thoughts of England's beauty and his own comparative unimportance, may not have been far away.

In the most obvious connection to the First World War, Thomas questions whether he should start to look elsewhere - towards death, perhaps - to find a similar beauty to the one that lies before him. The "small dark drops" on the "pale dust" laden path could be a reference to the drops of blood left by soldiers, who have taken this road before Thomas and found there the beauty, strength and happiness that Thomas also craves, even if it is only "short-lived". His assertion that those who remain safely at home in the "hazel copse" "know nought" of such happiness, seems to reinforce this connection to the war. This makes sense when the reader bears in mind how close Thomas was to deciding to enlist and how long he had taken to reach this conclusion. His had been a difficult road to enlistment, made more so by self-doubt and possibly by self-indulgence as to his own feelings and importance. Like Wilfred Owen, Thomas wondered for a time, whether his real duty lay in staying at home and perpetuating the language of his country through his writing, rather than fighting for it. Perhaps he was starting to believe in the inadequacy of this sentiment - as in the end, did Owen.

Next, Thomas questions whether, rather than seeking his "short-lived" happiness, he will have to remain discontented. This enlightens the reader as to Thomas's state of mind and his sense of unhappiness and lack of fulfilment. He likens this feeling to birds, who have to make do with only having wings: useful - necessary even, but are they everything a bird needs? This again may be representative of the notion that, while he has his words and his walks, which have always meant so much to him, these are no longer enough and he needs to find the missing links in his life to make it complete.

Thomas's next question is to ponder whether he will be able to decide what "happiness" is. His reference to "day's end" may actually mean "life's end". So, here he is perhaps wondering whether, at the end of his life, he will still be uncertain as to the real meaning of beauty and his own happiness, or role in it. He wonders next whether he will be willing - or able - to let go of life, beauty and and happiness, and whether, in doing so, he will finally have found contentment, or whether he will still continue to feel "weary" with the world.

Finally, Thomas considers whether, at the end, he will realise that he was actually happy at various times in the past; that he has forgotten his own capacity for withdrawing into himself rather to quickly and easily, not releasing himself again.

He comments that time - or the passage of it - is boring, when there is nothing to look forward to, which implies a certain pointlessness in doing nothing and suggests that he would prefer a definite course of action - whatever that might be - to indolence. Finally, he comments that, regardless of everything else, he is incapable of real enjoyment, or fulfilment: he cannot simply lose himself in the happiness, wonder and joy of life.

This is a sad poem in which we can easily see Thomas's depressive, somewhat self-obsessed personality, coupled with the fact that an enormous and momentous decision (about whether or not to enlist) lay upon his shoulders. The fact that he was not the only man to face such a decision, or that, either way, it would have dire consequences to those who loved him, seems not to have entered his head and, like many artistic people, his perspective is very self-centred. Thomas speaks only of his happiness and satisfaction; his own heart, his search for contentment. His language is focused on himself at all times and if he rarely does look elsewhere, it is not towards his devoted wife and family, but to nature and whatever she may offer him.

This poem could be compared to Thomas's *Melancholy*, written just a few days before *The Glory*, on 25th April 1915. Thomas creates in *Melancholy*, at atmosphere of sad self-absorption. He doesn't allow the war to intrude too far into his world, referring to it only in the form of "rumours", even though it is clearly taking up quite a lot of his thoughts. The tension of indecision here is palpable and is given an air of sweetness, which refers us back to the beauty and "happiness" for which he searches in *The Glory*. At the time, both seemed equally elusive: Thomas had no idea what his decision would be, with regard to the war, but the agony of being unable to decide was becoming tortuous. At the same time, in *The Glory*, we sense that his search for fulfilment in any other avenue is proving equally difficult, pushing him in the direction of enlistment, despite his fears for his own future, if he took that route. The ultimate sadness is within the final line of the piece where Thomas simply states that he cannot "bite the day to the core", or live life to the full: giving the impression of a man who has seen everything he wants and longs for; has held it in his grasp, but has rejected it, on the grounds that he feels there should be more; that something still is lacking and he craves that greater happiness which he hopes will be waiting around the corner, not realising that it is really right in front of him, if he would only take the bite.

WORDS

(Written 26-28 June 1915)

This is one of several poems included in the OCR A-Level syllabus, in which I find it difficult to perceive any obvious connections to the First World War. Edward Thomas is frequently classified, rightly or wrongly, as a war poet and, therefore, his poetry is seen as belonging, sometimes exclusively, to that genre. This is really a mistake, since Thomas never wrote a graphic or detailed war poem and did not write poetry at all once he had embarked for France. Several of his poems have the war as a background - albeit vague - but this is not an exclusive feature and many remain distinctly detached from the conflict. Nonetheless, this confusion and misinformation has led to Great War Literature Publishing receiving numerous requests to provide a complete series of analyses for the OCR selection, regardless of each poem's content, or the poet's intentions. Therefore, despite our misgivings, we have undertaken this task.

Words was written in late June 1915, only a couple of weeks before Thomas finally decided to enlist in the Artists Rifles. At this stage, however, he was certainly leaning more towards travelling to America to see if he could find a readier audience for his poetry. Thomas's son, Merfyn, was already in the United States, a guest of the family of American poet, Robert Frost, who had become a friend of Edward Thomas's when Frost and his family had lived in England during the previous three years. Whether Thomas would have travelled alone to join the Frosts and Merfyn, leaving his wife, Helen, and two daughters in England is now a matter of debate. He certainly had insufficient funds really to support his family in either circumstance, unless his poetry was successful in America, and the weight of family responsibility weighed heavily on his mind, as well as his pocket - although perhaps not his heart.

In June of 1915, Thomas went on a short cycling tour in Gloucestershire and Herefordshire, visiting May Hill, from where he could see into Wales. This was territory which Thomas had earlier visited with Robert Frost, thus bringing back memories of his now absent American friend. May Hill is commonly thought to have provided the setting for *Words*, but it also highlighted the quandary within the poet's mind: to go to America, or to enlist? By the middle of the following month, Thomas had decided on the latter course and, having passed his medical, had joined the Artists Rifles. Both Helen and Eleanor Farjeon (his admirer and the typist of his manuscripts, as well as a poet in her own right) would later comment that, once Thomas had made this decision, he seemed more settled and contented within himself.

The poem itself seems to focus in part around choices, perhaps reflecting the poet's state of mind. It opens with Thomas's question as to whether the "words" will choose him as a poet, to propagate their message. In this way, perhaps, he hopes to absolve himself from the responsibility, or possibly the guilt, of having to make a decision about the future, leaving that to the words - if they choose him, all well and good, he'll remain a poet: if not, he'll enlist. However, there could also be a question here about Thomas's confidence as a poet, as opposed to a writer of prose. At this stage, almost none of Thomas's poetry had been published and, that which had, had been done under the pseudonym of Edward Eastaway. This had been a deliberate choice on the part of Thomas, using his paternal grandfather's middle name to separate his poetry writing from his prose. Nonetheless, Thomas remained uncertain about his own abilities and prowess as a poet, following rejections of his manuscripts. Here, therefore, he could be asking that the words help him to decide whether he is a worthy poet and whether he should turn his back on the more lucrative reviews and critical prose writings of the past.

In this poem, Thomas likens the choice made by the words to a sort of inevitability, similar to the wind having to pass through a "crack in a wall", and yet there is an underlying sense of something unpleasant, or even sinister about this, despite his mentioning of the word "joy", since this is balanced with "pain", because Thomas reminds us that the wind merely whistles through the crack, not remaining for any time, but only passing by, on its way to, presumably, better things. Thomas also makes the point here, that his words are "English", reminding us, as he frequently does, of his patriotism and love for his country, even though we know that, at this time, he was seriously considering emigrating to the United States.

Thomas next asserts his more confident familiarity with words, commenting on their lightness and strength; their value and their sweetness. These adjectives are all apt in a general description of the use of the written word, which can achieve much (or little) if used wisely. Thomas likens words to some typically English aspects, such as the oak tree, the poppy, a field of corn, a rose in the height of summer, a bird singing. All of these may be enhanced by the use of appropriate words, which can, at the same time, be "light", allowing the reader as much, or as little input as they might wish. The writer can, therefore, wax lyrical on a topic, or tread gently and, if the right words are used, still achieve the same effect. This "strange" sweetness of words gives them a familiarity, making them seem similar to loved ones, or "lost homes". This passage could be argued as having a possible First World War connection, in that soldiers, far from home, might find themselves reminded of "dearest faces" and "lost homes" by familiar words, either in the form of a simple letter, or a great work of literature, bought with them from home. Both would feature words of different types and cultures, but would have the same value and purpose to the soldier. However, whether Thomas intended the reader to draw this conclusion from this section of the poem is another matter. He goes on to say, reinforcing his earlier comments, that it doesn't matter whether words are old or new - so, whether they come in the form of a simple note, a letter or a classical piece of prose or poetry, each word has a place in a man's heart.

In the next verse, Thomas makes mention of his Welsh heritage, of which he was very proud, commenting that the nightingales (birds which are renowned for their beautiful song - as are the Welsh people) "have no wings", meaning that they have no desire to leave their homeland. However, Thomas would also be "content", he says, with sweet words (or memories) from any number of the counties: Wiltshire, having been a childhood favourite; Kent, where he had lived when first married; or Herefordshire when he was when writing this poem.

Finally, Thomas asks a favour of the words: that he be permitted to "dance" with them, just occasionally; even sometimes, to join them "in ecstasy", in a poem, both "fixed and free" - an oxymoron which may easily be said to describe many forms of poetry. Thomas wishes to behave he says, "as poets do" - linked with words, in unbound happiness.

The form of this poem is interesting as Thomas has used very short lines - occasionally of one word only, sometimes with a simple rhyme pattern, sometimes with no rhyme at all. This forces the reader to focus on the words themselves, which must surely have been his intention, given the title and content of the poem.

Unlike many of Thomas's poems, there is actually a sense of happiness and fulfilment here and the reader can see that Thomas felt the greatest feeling of contentment in writing about his art. He may not have had the highest opinion of his own work (or maybe this was false modesty), but he had a very high view of the English language. Thomas certainly did not wish to see it perish or falter and, although this poem would seem to signal that Thomas had decided to remain a poet and not to enlist, he may have begun to decide that it was more important to take direct action to protect this important part of his heritage.

As with many of his other poems, Thomas makes direct references here to nature, especially to trees and birds, which always seem of great importance to him. Other examples of this include *But these things also*, in which Thomas mentions how the "chattering" starlings do their best to keep up the appearance that spring is approaching, even though they are a non-migrating bird and have actually been "chattering" all winter long, denoting really how man places false hopes and expectations on such events. In *The Glory*, Thomas speaks of the cuckoo, blackbird and dove, as well as the fields and forests, all of which remind him of his own sadness and shortcomings when compared to the wonders of nature. In *Words*, however, we have a rather different story, where Thomas doesn't seem so self-absorbed or depressed, but rather appears to be beginning to appreciate that there are things in life that are more important than his own decisions, perhaps because his own choice is made. He seems to have understood that poetry is a gift given to few to pass on; received and loved by many; and that he was, perhaps, becoming one of the blessed.

Aspens

(Written 11th July 1915)

This poem was written on July 11th 1915, just three days before Edward Thomas successfully took his army medical, prior to joining the Artists Rifles. This means that, by the time he wrote this poem, the great decision, as to whether to enlist, or emigrate to America, had already been made and this alters the tone of this poem from those which he had been writing while still undecided.

The setting for the poem is generally thought to be a cross-roads at Steep in Hampshire, where the poet lived. There, The Cricketer's Inn still stands and, having been there myself on a recent visit, during a fairly windy day, I can vouch for the noise that the trees make as their leaves are swept to and fro. Both Thomas and his great friend, Robert Frost, when he saw it, thought this poem to be among the poet's finest, and Frost's poem *The Sound of the Trees* (published the previous year) may have also provided some inspiration for Thomas. In his poem, Frost discusses the way in which man tolerates and, eventually joins in with, the noises and movements made by the trees, but that the trees will outlive the men. Thomas, however, was ultimately obliged to admit his poem's obscurity, in a letter to Eleanor Farjeon who, in typing out the manuscript, seems to have misunderstood Thomas's meaning, forcing him to write to her on July 21st to explain that, in fact, he had been the aspen and that "we" in the poem referred to both the trees and himself, with all his "dejected shyness". Despite this explanation, the poem remains relatively obscure, probably reflecting the poet's state of mind, having decided to enlist, but being still uncertain as to what lay ahead. Thomas disliked indecision and uncertainty, being made to feel uneasy and depressed by such thoughts. There are some connections to the First World War here, but also to Thomas's position as a poet, and to a sense of a lost history.

The poem opens with a reference to the trees that stand near to "the inn, the smithy, and the shop". These aspens, generally, would have been older (due to their height - they are "above" the buildings) and this type of tree can live for up to 150 years, although the root system of a colony of trees would be much older still. This is one of Thomas's main points in this poem: that people - like trees - put down roots in a community, which can go back over generations, but which may be torn up without sufficient care. Here, he comments that the trees all "talk" to each other, except in winter, when they have no leaves to make any sound. Their favourite topic is the rain, presumably because that is part of what keeps them alive - although this may also be a humorous reflection of the British obsession with the weather. Equally, it may be indicative of Thomas's own pre-occupation with rain, which he mentions in several other poems including *Rain*, *Blenheim Oranges* and *Melancholy*, among others. The trees surround an area which, containing the shop, the smithy and the inn, would have formed the hub of the community, so these buildings represent the people who would have gone about their daily business on the streets below.

This sense of village harmony and longevity is continued into the second verse, where Thomas explains that the sounds of the blacksmith's hammering and the revelry from the inn have been heard in the village for over fifty years. The human sounds have, therefore accompanied the natural ones, working in unison to form the whole community. The fact that Thomas placed himself with the trees, rather than the people, however, suggests that his "dejected shyness" was playing a part and that he preferred his natural surroundings, away from groups of people. He certainly was spending less and less time with his family at this stage of his life.

Unlike the human voices and noises, which come and go, the sounds of the trees cannot be "drowned" out, either literally or metaphorically. Even when the humans have all gone, the trees will carry one "talking", regardless of how "empty" the earth becomes. These are the first real references to the war, as Thomas begins to make us realise that the men who had previously used or worked at the smithy and who had drunk at the inn are no longer there. These places are now "silent": the men are now "ghosts", summoned unsuccessfully by the calling trees. Thomas makes a references to the fact that it matters not whether it is a bright night with "bare moonlight", or a foggy "thick-furred gloom"; a "tempest" of a wind may be blowing, or it may be peaceful enough to hear the nightingale sing - either way the trees and the lack of men are capable of turning the "cross-roads" into a ghoulish place. He refers to this as a "room", implying that it has walls, imposed by the high trees, surrounding the area.

In the fifth verse, Thomas goes on to point out that the feeling would be identical, even if no-one had ever lived nearby: it would still feel as if the trees were the only things left to "speak", although we must remember that Thomas counts himself as one of the trees, meaning he also has somethng to say. Some men still live, but have, it would seem, gone dumb - or at least have nothing valuable to say - and despite the aspen's noise, Thomas asserts that no-one is listening. They can hear, but they do not listen, or at least, they pay no more attention to the trees than they do to Thomas's poetry. This may be a reflection of the fact that, at the time, Thomas's poems remained largely unpublished - certainly in his own name - this explains his dejection as he presumably felt his valuable words were being ignored. Nonetheless, he asserts that while he and the aspens have breath (in the case of the trees, in the form of the wind), they will continue to speak, even if no-one listens. He believes that others might find the sounds of the aspens (and, therefore, him) mournful, but he says this should only apply to other trees, or poets.

Thomas wrote complex, multi-faceted poems, often with several explanations, but one which certainly strikes me as appropriate here is that, (once one has realised that the poet had likened himself to the aspens and that he was writing about himself in terms of poetry), one can understand that this is a poem in which he is describing the experience of writing something which no-one reads and in which no-one is interested. There are war connections, in part because Thomas was not writing the same type of "war poetry" (if one can classify his work within that genre at all) as others at this stage. In 1915, The public was lapping up poems by Rupert Brooke, Laurence Binyon, Julian Grenfell, Wilfrid Wilson Gibson and even Jessie Pope and, they and others were being widely published in magazines, newspapers and anthologies, while Thomas wasn't. Therefore, his poetry was falling largely on deaf ears, even though, as a critic before the war, he had helped to make the names of many of those who were now rising above him: a situation which he deeply resented. He had also associated easily with many of the now famous war poets - especially those in the "Dymock" group, which included his friend Robert Frost, as well as Brooke and Gibson and together they may have originally seemed to Thomas like a group of trees, whispering their great words to the expectant ears below them. Now, however, the ears did not always wish to hear his words, because he was no longer singing the right tune. Thomas's poetry remained firmly set in the natural world, while others of the group - even the non-combatants, like Gibson, were writing trench poetry, or patriotic verse, like that of Rupert Brooke.

In this case, the grief which Thomas mentions would be for the loss of a way of life that the aspens - and he - have witnessed for many years. He says that the inn, the smithy and the shop are "empty", having been full of life for "these fifty years". The men have gone away to war, and to death and Thomas senses that the rural way of life will never return to its former glories. This same message can be seen in Thomas's poem *As the Team's Head-Brass*, in which he compares the death and destruction of the war, with the way in which nature has the strength to continue and thrive. Thomas worried about the future of his country and the traditions that he had grown to love and both of these poems reflect his fears.

THIS IS NO CASE OF PETTY RIGHT OR WRONG

(Written 26th December 1915)

This poem was written on 26th December 1915, at which stage, Edward Thomas had been serving in the army for just over six months. At this time, he was still based at Hare Hall, Gidea Park in Essex, where he worked as a map reading instructor. The basis for this poem appears to have been that Thomas was thinking back to the beginning of the war, when he was contemplating enlisting, but was undecided due to his feelings of patriotism and duty towards his country; his sense of responsibility for his family and his desire to pursue his literary career, probably in the United States. At the same time as revisiting his original decision regarding his enlistment, Thomas may also have begun to wonder about his current position in the war, pondering whether his service in England was enough or whether he should volunteer for an overseas posting.

This poem opens with the affirmation that the war is not so simple as the rhetoric of the politicians and philosophers would have us believe. Thomas appears to criticise those who are attempting to heighten nationalistic fervour by creating a hatred and distrust of the German people as a whole. He sees the guilty parties here as the newspapers, and those who spout patriotism, while doing nothing to help the country themselves - thus their indolence has made them "fat" or complacent.

He tells us that he feels more hatred towards these so-called patriots, who are in fact more like parasites sucking the life out of the nation, than he does towards the Kaiser himself. He seems to believe that the Kaiser has almost deified himself, and calls his nation to arms to protect their way of life. Thomas was not anti-German, despite his love of England, and found that his frequent arguments on this subject with those who found Germans abhorrent, caused great friction.

Then he points out that it is not his place to decide between the corpulent patriots and the Kaiser. He feels as though he has been deafened by the clamour of war, and cannot make sense of any more of the arguments for or against. He feels confused and compares this confusion with trees in a storm, surrounded by the blowing, howling wind and unable to escape from the cacophony. These storms could be a metaphor for the uproars of battle; the smoke having been caused by the guns on the battlefield.

Into all this seemingly endless noise, he adds the "roar" of witches' cauldrons. This could be an allusion to *Macbeth* by William Shakespeare, in which the witches first appear in the midst of a terrible thunderstorm and speak of meeting with Macbeth "when the hurlyburly's done,/When the battle's lost and won." These witches can predict the future and although their initial tidings for Macbeth appear promising, their fulfilment ultimately brings about his downfall. Thomas's cauldrons predict a rosy future, fair and beautiful, yet he reminds us that in order to bring about this idyllic image, the old England must die.

Thomas says that he does not care whether, in the future, historians are able to fathom a reason for the conflict, as, by that stage, England - unsurpassed in beauty - will have risen from the ashes of self-destruction and be serene once more. This reference to the myth of the phoenix rising from the ashes brings to mind the notion that England will survive the destruction of war, in some shape or form. Such hope for serenity has a greater value to Thomas than the historian's knowledge or understanding. He is implying that the reasons for the war, are themselves, unimportant.

In another Shakespearean reference, reminiscent of the patriotic speeches of Henry V, the poet states that he stands, as one, with every true Englishman, in his desire to save his country, for such a loss could never be recovered. It is as though he believes himself to be joined with his country and he is comforted by his familiarity with it and by its innate goodness. He avers that if such a love for one's country and a desire to protect it necessitate a hatred of the enemy, then so be it: for as much as he does not love all Englishmen, or hate all Germans, his love for England and wish for its preservation is paramount. It is worth noting that he does not perceive the enemy as his enemy, but England's.

Written at the end of 1915, after Thomas had enlisted, this poem was, almost certainly, a means of justifying (even if only to himself) his decision to enter the war. He feels that the necessity to defeat the enemy and protect his beloved England, is more important than any protestations of politicians, philosophers, journalists or historians. He is also being critical of those who use more jingoistic and nationalistic cries to further their own cause.

This poem could also be interpreted as a criticism of the other poets and writers, whose calls to arms were regularly published at this time. He had, at one stage, been publicly critical of Rupert Brooke's poems, accusing him of arrogance and self-promotion. This, despite the fact that he and Brooke had both been members of the small band of Georgian poets, known as the Dymock Group, demonstrates that to Thomas, the war was not about men and deeds, but about preserving the future of England.

The tone of this poem, like much of Thomas's work, is patriotic, with a reference to his country, rather than the war and is, in some ways, similar to Julian Grenfell's *Into Battle*. Both poems praise the idea of protecting one's country and fighting for what is held dear. In contrast to Thomas's poem, however, Grenfell writes very much from a soldier's perspective: a soldier, that is, who firmly believes in the righteousness of his cause. Grenfell had little time for those who would not fight, believing them to be as good as dead. *Into Battle* affirms Grenfell's belief that those who die fighting for their country and for what they believe in, will, of necessity, be greater and better than those who refuse to fight. Thomas does not seem to agree with this philosophy. To him the heroic nature of the deed is of minimal importance compared to the continuation of the way of life which he holds so dear.

This poem has a more optimistic tone than *As the Team's Head Brass*, for example. Here, in *Petty*, there are fewer negative images, England being portrayed as virtuous and beautiful, and worthy of salvation, while in *Head-Brass*, the consequences of war are shown to be more negativeand irreparable.

Rain

(Written 7th January 1916)

This is a complex and complicated poem which requires some fairly detailed understanding of the poet's background and his sensibilities, as well as the concept that someone who is suffering from depression - as Thomas frequently did - does not see things from the same perspective as others might. Depression takes many forms: Winston Churchill used to call his a "black dog", which seems a bizarre, even slightly friendly description for something that is so consuming and destructive. To those who have never been depressed, it often seems as though the sufferer has simply given up and cannot be bothered to 'get a grip'. This is not the case: they are not capable of taking control. It would appear that Thomas displayed the typical symptoms of depression throughout most of his adult life, some of which are reflected in this poem.

In the late summer of 1911, Edward Thomas had written a prose account of his feelings while lying in the dark, listening to the rain. This account can be found in his book *The Icknield Way*, which was published in 1913. In this passage, Thomas creates a dull and depressing atmosphere of a rain storm: not as something which cleanses and refreshes, as storms often do, but as something which destroys everything, including both "life and death". The account is very dark, showing not only the extreme stress that Thomas was under at the time he wrote it, but also the effect which the weather, especially when prolonged and unremitting, can have of someone of his sensibilities. He speaks of himself as being overwhelmed by the enormity of the rain, which absorbs or "swallows" everything in its wake, making him feel "little" and "forgotten", as though he were "never alive". He ends the piece acknowledging the "full truth of the words I used to love... in the days before the rain: 'Blessed are the dead that the rain rains on.'" So, although the rain he is describing is destructive, he can still recall a time when it served a different, and better, purpose, making his rain, possibly symbolic: a metaphor for anything that consumes completely and wantonly.

This passage and the knowledge of it, provide invaluable background information when examining Thomas's poem, Rain and, indeed, it is hard to see how one can hope to fully appreciate the poem without knowing of the prose account. Rain was written very early in 1916, while Thomas was still at Hare Hall, Gidea Park, in Essex, where he worked as a map reading instructor, having been promoted to the rank of Lance-Corporal in November 1915. Throughout his life, Thomas had been plagued by frequent and worsening bouts of depression and would often take himself off into the countryside - sometimes for days on end - to avoid being confined by family life.

Rain is clearly a poem written by a depressed person, made obvious by the fact that Thomas writes about himself as though he were dead and wishes that state upon himself. He refers to his life as a "solitude" and to his state as "solitary"; comments that he realises he is going to die, which might be more easily understood if he were writing this while lying in a trench or a dugout with shells screaming overhead, rather than in a hut in Essex, before Thomas had decided to apply for a posting overseas. There is also desolation as he can hear "nothing but the wild rain" and even his position, although safe in reality, is "bleak", showing that he can see no future for himself. He anticipates that when he is dead, he won't be able to hear the rain, or to thank it for cleansing him. Many poets saw the rain as having cleansing powers and here, Thomas seems to believe that it has the properties to remove all of his impurities and return him to the innocence of birth, when he was "born into this solitude". He seems to feel as though no-one shares or understands the depths of his despair or loneliness.

Next, Thomas repeats the line from his prose account of the rain storm, written five years earlier: "Blessed are the dead that the rain rains upon", which was a popular West Country superstition, meaning that if it rained on a coffin at a funeral, then the soul of the departed had arrived safely in Heaven. However, not being dead yet, Thomas hopes - prays even - that no-one whom he "once... loved" is either dying or lying in the same predicament as himself: feeling sympathetic, yet "helpless" towards both the living and those who will die, in other words, apathetic. The "broken reeds", which represent those who are waiting to die, have ceased to exist in their previous form: they don't wave in the breeze like they should, but are just "still and stiff", which again, Thomas says, is how he feels. So, not only is he like the "cold water", floating without purpose or feeling among the "broken reeds" - or the men waiting to die - but he is also a "broken reed" himself, since he anticipates his own death.

All his love is gone, he says, except his love for death, because that is the only love which the "wild rain" has not "dissolved". At the end of the poem, Thomas seems to imply that a love of death is the only "perfect" love, which can never "disappoint" and it could be interpreted that not only does he love death, but it loves him back. This final couplet may be a reference to Shakespeare's *Sonnet Number 116*, in which he states the firmness and strength of love, which can, if strong enough, withstand any "tempests and is never shaken", even if that tempest be the passage of time or beauty; a change in circumstances or even the infidelity of one or other of the parties. Shakespeare goes on to say that, if he be proved wrong in his assertions about love, then "I never writ, nor no man ever loved.", so heartfelt are his feelings on the subject of the strength of true love. Thomas, however, seems prepared to argue this point, to a degree at least, since his strongest love is not for a woman, but for death, in which he finds nothing to "disappoint", even when he looks for approval to the "tempests", which Shakespeare had urged him could only strengthen human love. In finding this approbation from the "tempests", or the worst that life has to offer, we must assume that the love of death makes Thomas, somehow, more complete than any other love he has experienced.

Although we do not know exactly what form of depression Edward Thomas suffered from, we do know, from various biographies, that it manifested itself in self-doubt, feelings of insecurity, the need for periods of solitude, mood changes, restlessness and violent outbursts. This poem reads as though, when writing, Thomas was in a dark place, where he could see no value to his existence. He perceives himself as either already dead, or useless and no better than a "broken reed". He also assumes himself to be unloved: "Like me who have no love", since this description may apply not only to the love he feels, but also to the love he thinks he receives. By extension, this must also mean that he believes that the only thing that does love him is death. This assumption is blatantly untrue and unfair, as Helen's love for him, though frequently tested, never faltered, and she remained loyal and true to him, even after his death. The thought process, however, is typical of someone in the depths of depression, who cannot see any reason why anyone should love them, making death seem like rather an attractive alternative.

The desolation in this poem is consuming and I have rarely read anything so depressing within this genre. The poet's numb acceptance of death does not mask his feelings of pity for those who might be "dying tonight", although he qualifies this, as he only seems concerned for people that he had once loved, making this quite a selfish pity. This propensity for putting everything that is positive into the past and dwelling only on the negative may smack a little of self-pity, especially when one bears in mind that he was writing in complete safety. If the piece had been written in peacetime, one's interpretation would be entirely different and one could assess the poem purely from the perspective of the poet's depression. However, although the depression must be accommodated, the poem still feels a little self-indulgent, considering the hell that others were going through at the time.

Thomas looks at everything in this poem only from his own viewpoint: "I shall die"; "washing me cleaner than I have been/ Since I was born"; "here I pray that none whom once I loved"; "like me who have no love", etc. This suggests self absorption, wallowing in his own experiences, which at this point, didn't really amount to anything very significant, compared with those of many of his fellow countrymen. It could be argued, therefore, that the poem reveals another thought process: we might question whether this period marked the beginning of Thomas's doubts about his own role in the conflict. Was he wondering whether he should be doing more and what might be the consequences of such a decision? The loneliness of the one not participating fully in the war may be a mark of his "solitude". Is his "helplessness" caused by the fact that he knows his death, of which he feels assured, will ultimately make no difference and that he will become just another sacrifice? It is worth remembering that, although Thomas felt a responsibility towards his wife and children, his love for his country may well have been the guiding force behind the decision as to whether to risk everything overseas, or stay safely in Essex. Nonetheless, even this abiding love of country was not the "perfect" love he, perhaps, craved: it had proved disappointing. He possibly sensed that his love was very one-sided; that England did not love her soldiers as she might have done; that those at home, for whom sacrifices were being made, did not always appreciate the hardships of those who fought. When he had enlisted in July 1915, Thomas had described his feelings and reasons for fighting, as follows:

"It seemed to me that either I had never loved England, or I had loved it foolishly, aesthetically, like a slave, not having realised that it was not mine, unless I were willing and prepared to die rather than leave it."

Perhaps, as he began to contemplate applying for a commission and a posting overseas, or at least questioning his role in the conflict, the idea of leaving and dying for his country was beginning to become a reality. It is also possible that in Rain he is asking himself some of these profound questions: is his love for his country that perfect love, or does it disappoint? Is it unrequited, or is it returned as fully as it is given? If it disappoints, then the only thing really left for him is death, since to live on, "helpless" and "broken" by his shattered dreams, would be so much worse.

NO ONE SO MUCH AS YOU (M.E.T.)

(Written 11th February 1916)

Although this poem is generally known by its first line, it also has a subtitle of (M.E.T.), which gives away the person to whom the poem is addressed, as the poet's mother - Mary Elizabeth Thomas (or Townsend, to use her maiden name). This piece was written in February 1916, while Edward Thomas was training close to London, spending a great deal of time with his parents at their home at Balham in London. Shortly before writing this piece, Thomas had also written a poem addressed to his father, which has a very different tone altogether, made obvious by its title: *I may come near loving you*, which tells a rather damning version of the relationship between the two men. The oldest of six sons, most of whom followed their father into clerical or civil service work, Edward Thomas had gone against his father's wishes when he chose to become a writer. Then, when Thomas enlisted as a private soldier, this also did not find favour with his father, who often tried to persuade his son to apply for a commission. When Thomas initially refused this, his father became openly critical of Thomas's poetry, which may well have led to him writing his verse, ending: "But not so long as you live/ Can I love you at all.", which is a sad indictment on their relationship. This strain was not reflected in the connection between Thomas and his mother, who remained close, presumably her expectations being less exacting. Therefore, within days, Thomas wrote a poem full of admiration, aimed at his mother. Eventually, of course, Thomas would succumb and apply for a commission in the Royal Garrison Artillery, but that decision was still many months away at the time he wrote the poems addressed to his parents.

This poem opens with the poet's acknowledgement that his mother loves his country just as much as he does and would feel just as sad as him, if it were to suffer or perish. This could well be a thinly veiled criticism of Thomas's father, who may well have doubted his son's patriotism for declining a commission and remaining safely in England, rather than taking an overseas posting. In this opening verse, rather like a child who has been scolded by one parent, Thomas perhaps looks to the other for reassurance.

In the second verse, Thomas goes on to concede that his mother knows him well and, even though he tells her nothing directly, she still understands him. Despite this understanding, however, she is not made brave at all. In other words, her superior knowledge of her son does nothing for her: it doesn't make her strong enough to face the consequences of what might happen to Thomas if he takes a commission and goes overseas. Again, this could be a concealed censure of Thomas's father's attitude, which the poet might have perceived as being somewhat cavalier, and not taking into consideration the feelings of others - such as his mother. This verse also tells us that Thomas is not good at communicating: he tells his mother nothing, possibly because there is nothing to tell, but maybe because he chooses to keep his feelings and thoughts to himself.

Next, Thomas goes on to praise his mother even more personally, referring to her as the fairest - or most beautiful - person he has ever known. It is unlikely that, in this instance, he is using the word "fair" to signify reasonable or trustworthy, because he would be more likely to use the word in its poetic or archaic form, but also because he had previously commented in his autobiography *The Childhood of Edward Thomas*, how physically attractive he found his mother to be. Her appeal is so strong for him that he cannot stand to hear anyone speak out in opposition to her. This attitude seems quite possessive, or possibly obsessive, especially when compared with Thomas's derogatory opinion of his father's "impotence", which type of insult he would clearly not permit to be made against his mother.

Thomas then begins to criticise himself, although he really does this as another means of praising his mother, stating that he thinks his actions towards her have always appeared uncouth. He has always hidden his true feelings from her, showing only a more crass side to his nature. Again, in his autobiography, Thomas had earlier recalled that, although he had liked to please his mother, he had also often found himself being "deceitful" towards her, which left him in a quandary. This doubt, voiced in verse five, leads him to wonder why he sometimes cannot bring himself to even look at his mother. He ponders whether his feelings for his mother are really love, or just the natural response of a son to his mother. There seems to be a real fear here, as though he genuinely doesn't understand the true nature of his feelings and we sense that he finds this thought quite disturbing.

Thomas then acknowledges that the words which he and his mother exchange hold no great significance: this is reserved for the way in which they "look" at one another - only in this manner can they truly "understand". He refers to their words as "weak" suggesting that they are not so important or meaningful as their actions, which may suggest that they find it difficult to verbally acknowledge the truth of Thomas's situation, in that, if he goes overseas, he might die. They do not mention this terrible reality, but speak instead of "trifles", presumably afraid to mention the truth.

In the final four verses of the poem, which actually form one long sentence, Thomas reiterates his own feelings of inadequacy with regard to his mother. She loves him, he says, but all that he can do in return is to "accept" her feelings for him and regret that he cannot return them in kind. In the meanwhile, he acknowledges that, while her love for him - her firstborn child - might make her "burn" with emotion, his feelings are much less intense. This makes him feel so beneath her that he wonders if he would be better off not seeing her at all, rather than lingering on as he does now. This feeling may have been exacerbated by the fact that Thomas had recently been unwell and had been forced, therefore, to spend some additional time at his parent's house, possible prolonging his existing feelings of awkwardness. This was almost certainly made worse by his poor relationship with his father, which we can easily imagine causing a difficult atmosphere within the house, perhaps causing Thomas's mother into many unpleasant situations, maybe dividing her loyalties, about which Thomas may well have felt responsible and guilty. He goes on to mention his "gratitude" towards his mother, but says he feels this "instead of love", which is damning praise for a mother to hear. Finally, he refers to himself as a "pine", which could be the poet using a verb in place of a noun, meaning that he "pines" to feel love for his mother, but cannot. He describes himself as "in solitude", which is not at all unusual for an Edward Thomas poem, in which he often seems to see himself as a solitary, sometimes even abandoned figure. We sense that, on this occasion, Thomas's "solitude" brings with it some sadness. In this instance, he is also "cradling a dove", which we could take to represent a peace offering, possibly for the conflict which he has caused within the family home, and for any upset that this might have brought upon his mother.

This is a poem which features some half-rhyme (as in "through"/"know" and "prove"/"love"). However, in verse nine only, Thomas changes the rhyme pattern completely, from abab to abbb, while also using half-rhyme: "were"/"more"/"here". This changes the tone and emphasis of the poem, since it is at this point that the poet mentions that it might be easier not to see his mother at all, rather than having to speak of their feelings. This change causes the reader - even if only subconsciously - to consider the importance of Thomas's meaning at this moment: the significance of him saying that he would prefer not to discuss how he feels, to the point where, if necessary, he will avoid seeing his mother, even though he has already acknowledged that she is the only person who really understands him. The metre of the poem is irregular throughout, however, so the reader cannot embrace any sense of rhythm within the piece. We have to assume that all of this has been done intentionally to replicate the poet's feelings of uneasiness and the imbalance between the emotions of the people concerned.

To look at this poem in isolation does seem a little short-sighted, given that only days earlier, Thomas had written such a damning piece aimed directly at his father, while this poem offers only praise of his mother. He does not declare love for either parent, but he clearly admires and respects his mother for everything she has done, while his father receives only condemnation. Thomas was obviously troubled over his relationships with both parents. With his father, there were evidently problems relating to Thomas's perception of his father's lack of support and their differences of opinion over the war. On his mother's side, however, the feelings are reversed and, if anyone is shown to be inadequate, in Thomas's eyes, it is himself. Nonetheless, this poem is studied in isolation because students of the OCR syllabus in the UK are not required to examine the poem addressed to Thomas's father, which shows a fairly typical lack of knowledge and understanding on the part of the examining board, who have missed the opportunity to allow students the chance to examine the balanced paternal perspectives of this poet.

In February 1916, when this poem was written, Thomas was in training, having already been stationed at Hare Hall, Gidea Park in Essex, as a map reading instructor. In July 1916, he was offered a permanent position back at Hare Hall, which he declined, presumably because he was already contemplating applying for a commission, which he did in September. The real difficulty in February, however, was that Thomas's father wanted him to take a specific course of action (applying for a commission and overseas posting) for which, at that moment, Thomas was not ready. He seems to have blamed his father for the ensuing awkward situation, voiced specifically in the poem which he addressed to him. However, in this poem, addressed to his mother, Thomas seems to bear some of the responsibility himself, acknowledging that his feelings are not what they ought to be and that this may be the cause of some of the friction. There are undertones of guilt here, which are certainly not present in the poem to his father, suggesting that Thomas feels that his mother has been caught up in a situation not of her making, about which he could do something to make amends, if he were only prepared to show his feelings.

Interestingly, within two months of writing this poem, in April 1916, Thomas also wrote four more pieces, addressed to his three children and his wife, Helen. The ones to his children are, essentially about what he hopes the future will bring for them. However, although along similar lines, the one to Helen is much more intimate and revealing, showing us that Thomas understood his own inadequacies, which he also touches upon in this earlier poem addressed to his mother. He says that, given the opportunity, he would give Helen "As many children as your heart/Might wish for"; "all you have lost... or given to me"; and "I would give you back yourself". At the very close of the poem, he ends by saying that, if he could, he would give her his heart "if I could find/Where it lay hidden and it proved kind." He must have realised that he had made life difficult for Helen - as he had for his mother - and that she had born these troubles without complaint. In both cases, he was not ungrateful and maybe it was enough.

THE CHERRY TREES

(Written 7th-8th May 1916)

This poem was in May 1916, possibly as a recollection of the sights which Edward Thomas might well have witnessed on one of his many solitary walks that he used to take in the countryside around his home at Steep, near Petersfield in Hampshire. Thomas, at the time of writing, had recently been granted leave from Hare Hall, at Gidea Park in Essex, where he had been acting as a map-reading instructor. During this time, Thomas was making the difficult decision as to whether to remain at Hare Hall in safety, or to apply for a Commission and seek a posting overseas. He eventually chose the latter and, by November 1916, he had undergone his training and been transferred to 244 Siege Battery, Royal Garrison Artillery, as a Second Lieutenant.

Poems such as this seem to represent the poet's attempts to come to terms with the cost of war: both from a personal perspective and looking at the cost to the natural world. This was a theme to which Edward Thomas frequently returned, as can be seen in other poems, such as *In Memoriam (Easter 1915)* and anthologists, like Jon Stallworthy, often place these two poems side by side, assuming that they were written at similar times, despite the many months that elapsed between their compositions, showing the seriousness with which Edward Thomas treated this topic.

In this poem, Thomas writes of simple "Cherry Trees" which are so heavily laden with blossom that their branches "bend over". This gives us a metaphor for new life springing up, as well as the image of bounty - almost to the point of surfeit - leaving us to wonder whether the trees will be able to support all the fruit that will follow in the wake of the blossom, or whether the weight will be too much and will break the boughs. As such, this could be taken as an analogy for the destruction of the war: perhaps Edward Thomas is questioning whether the country, represented by the trees, can take the weight of the losses it is having to bear, or whether it will also break under the strain. The blossom, or "petals" are being dropped by the trees onto an "old road", implying that the trees have no use for the blossom, but also that the "old road" won't either, since it is barren, or infertile land, on which nothing can grow, making this a hopeless scene. This notion is reinforced by the statement that "all that passed" along the road "are dead", by which we may assume that soldiers have marched to war along this route, but have since died. We may, perhaps, infer that the men of a local village have all volunteered together, or maybe that the village has witnessed the passing of a regular BEF unit at the beginning of the war, which has since perished. Bearing in mind that this poem was written in the late spring or early summer of 1916, it pre-dates the Battle of the Somme, which saw the demise of so many volunteer "Pals" battalions, so although either of these situations is possible, the latter is, perhaps, more likely.

The "petals" that have fallen from the tree cover the grass "as for a wedding", creating an image of flowers that have been scattered, traditionally, at the feet of a bride and groom. This scene is one of great happiness and hope for the future, which Thomas enhances further, describing the day as an "early May morn", thereby reminding the reader not only that there might still be such weddings happening somewhere in the countryside, but also of the changing seasons. However, he immediately dashes this sense of hopefulness, pointing out that "there is none to wed", presumably because - as he has already told us - "all that passed are dead".

This, like Thomas's earlier poem *In Memoriam (Easter 1915)*, is a sad and mournful reflection, detailing the loss, not only of life, but also of a way of life. The men who would have walked down this road on their wedding day, are now dead; the women, therefore, have no-one to marry, so their lives are materially altered; their expectations lowered. Additionally, future generations must also be affected, because the young men have died, so they will not marry and have children, which metaphor is represented by the blossom being discarded, or abandoned by the tree and falling onto a barren road where nothing can grow. Finally, the rural landscape is altered, as there is no-one left to tend the land, depicted by the imagery of the bent and potentially broken trees.

Thomas's language is deliberately melancholy. Although he writes of blossom and weddings, he does not want the reader to harbour any feelings of optimism, so he couples cheerful words with cleverly placed pessimistic ones. For example, he rhymes "shedding" with "wedding", the latter being a positive event, bringing hope for the future, new life and cheerfulness; the former being a metaphor for discarding or abandoning something which is no longer required. In this instance, the thing being discarded is the blossom, which Thomas had used to represent new life and growth. So, these contradictory terms, juxtaposed in their rhymes, reinforce the message that all hope for the future is now lost. Thomas then goes on to repeat this exact process, rhyming "dead" with "wed", to the same effect.

The image created here is one of a rural idyll, gone awry, but not through natural causes. Man has made the petals fall, and the boughs bend, the roads barren and the women unwedded. As such, this makes Thomas's sadness all the more profound, as one senses that he feels something could (and should) have been done to prevent this situation; this end. If the causes had been natural, he might have found it easier to accept and had less grounds for his melancholy. As it is, his regrets are more earnest, perhaps, because he feels - at least in part - responsible.

THE SUN USED TO SHINE

(Written 22md May 1916)

This poem was written in mid-May 1916, following the receipt by Edward
Thomas of a letter from his close friend, the American poet, Robert Frost, who
had not written to Thomas since the beginning of March. This long silence and
Frost's letter prompted Thomas to recall a holiday which the two families had
spent together before the Frosts had returned to America in early 1915. This
holiday, which took place in August 1914 at Ledington in Herefordshire,
coincided with the beginning of the war. During this time, the two poets, who
shared a love of the countryside, took frequent walks together and that is the
memory, coupled with the recollection of the impending doom of war, that
prompted the writing of this poem. Even at this early stage of the conflict,
Thomas was undecided as to what he should do and Frost was urging his friend
to take his family to safety in America, where he was intended to return shortly
with his own wife and children. Indeed, a great many of the ensuing weeks
were spent with the Frosts at Ledington, while Thomas planned his possible
move to the US. Eventually, only Thomas's eldest son, Merfyn, made the trans-
Atlantic journey, as Thomas clearly had a change of heart and decided to enlist in
July 1915.

The opening of this poem portrays an image of two companions who seem very
contented in each other's company. They are clearly sufficiently comfortable that
they don't need to communicate in order to know what the other person wishes
to do. This scene might lead some readers to wonder whether the poet is
describing his relationship with his wife, although this is not, in fact, that case
and provides quite a telling indictment of the poet's marriage. It would seem that
Thomas possibly felt more at ease and maybe more intellectually intimate with
Frost than with his wife, Helen, whom he might not have seen as his equal on

that level. The future ("the to be") and the "late past" are of no interest to these two men, who discuss everything from other people - possibly in the form of gossip - to poetry and "rumours" that they have heard about the war, which Thomas describes as "remote", presumably demonstrating that, at this early stage of the conflict, the war didn't really have too much of an impact on either man. This, and the fact that they only hear "rumours" gives the war a feeling of unreality, as though it cannot touch their world, and certainly not if they don't allow the "rumours" to become facts. Thomas recalls that they talked together, until the only thing left for them to discuss was their own immediate surroundings, such as a yellowed apple, presumably fallen from a tree due to its colour, that has been damaged by wasps, hungry for its sweetness; a row of dark green mint ("betonies") that stand at the edge of the "forest verge"; crocuses which form a "pale purple" carpet, creating an impression that the fields, which should be lush and green, are actually much darker and more sinister, like something out of the underworld - "Hades" being the god of the underworld.

Next, however, the men are reminded of the war, as the sun sets and the moon rises, which makes them realise that the soldiers in the "east" (the battlefields would have been, geographically to the east of where Thomas and Frost were at the time) would have been looking at the exact same moon at the same time. Although they momentarily think of these soldiers, they also recall earlier conflicts, such as the Crusades or the Roman wars, remembering that, with the passage of time, those battles, although "glittering" and important at the time, had soon faded into nothing more than memories. They also realise that everything will go the same way: their own friendship and memories will soon become something that other men talk about as recollections or remembrances. Just as the sea comes and covers the sand each day, so their lives will soon be only a memory and they will be replaced by "other men" who will look upon the flowers and talk, and have peace, just as Thomas and Frost have done. This ending may also be a reference to the fact that, in fields on the Western Front, Thomas is aware that men are creating memories that will soon fade as well, leaving behind - he hopes - something more peaceful.

This poem is a mixture of happy, fond memories, mingled with sadness, as the poet realises that the life which he cherishes is transient and that nothing is ever going to be the same again, because of the war. By the time Thomas wrote this poem, Frost had already been back in America for over one year and Thomas himself was already contemplating applying for an overseas posting, which he felt certain would culminate in his own death. Whether he survived or not, this happy time could never again be replicated, as Thomas sensed that both he and his England would be changed forever by their experiences of the war.

There is a great feeling of familiarity here, not just between the two companions, who clearly share so much, but also between the poet and his surroundings, which he describes with great affection. Additionally, Thomas places great emphasis on the fact that nothing is really very significant: not himself or the passing seasons (represented by the "fallen apples"), or the war, because eventually everything becomes just a memory. He thinks that "other men" and "other flowers" will take his place, wherever they are, and we may assume that he is also implying here that there will also be other wars for men to fight. He refers to this time as "easy hours", which seems a very peaceful description of the time he has spent with Frost and allows the reader to realise the importance of that period of time for Thomas. He was really about to face some difficult decisions and, looking back from May 1916, those last days of tranquility, before he had to start focusing on the choices ahead, must have seemed almost heavenly.

The poem features a regular rhyme pattern, through which Thomas allows the reader to focus on his wording and phrases, which are both lyrical and flowing, reflecting the significance of the subject matter. Although Thomas had only known Frost since October 1913, so less than a year when the scene described in the poem was taking place, Frost's influence over Thomas was enormous, since it was he who inspired Thomas to begin writing poetry in the first place. In August 1914, when the holiday and walks described here took place, Thomas hadn't actually written any poetry at all, and wouldn't do so until December of that year. By May 1916, when he did write this piece, almost all of Thomas's poems were completed (all but the last twenty-five), so we can see how rapid was his development and how much he felt he owed to Frost.

No one cares less than I

(Written 25th-26th May 1916)

This poem was written right at the end of May 1916. By this stage, Thomas - who was serving in England as a map reading instructor - had probably already decided to apply for a commission, which would - he knew - involve an overseas posting. This application went through the following month. No one cares less than I is also known by the title of *Bugle Call* and is one of the poet's more obvious "war poems", since it actually features a definite war content and is based on his experiences at army camps.

The poem is also greatly influenced by two of the five *1914 Sonnets* written by Rupert Brooke, whom Thomas had known quite well before the war - the two men having first met in 1910. Thomas had also posthumously reviewed Brooke's sonnets more than once, but remained unconvinced as to their content and the poet's true abilities. Here, he is attempting a parody of Brooke's sonnets, based around his perception of a soldier's perspective of the "bugle call".

The poem opens with very obvious references to Brooke's sonnet *The Soldier* in which he states: "If I should die, think only this of me: / That there's some corner of a foreign field / That is forever England." While Brooke is full of patriotism and evident concern for his own future wellbeing, Thomas's attitude seems very different. He points out that "no one" is really very interested - especially not him - in whether he lives or dies. The only person who knows what will happen to him is God, but he's obviously not telling. These words are the ones which Thomas says he calls out to the bugle in the morning as it summons him to reluctantly awaken, showing that he senses a lack of interest from others in what might happen to him, but also that he is beyond caring himself. This contrasts greatly with the sentiments expressed by Brooke, who had been accused (by Charles Hamilton Sorley among others), of being a little too absorbed by his own sacrifices.

In the second verse, Thomas points out that the bugles mock the men, making them feel worthless. No one understands what their calls mean - except the bugles themselves: and even they don't care. This verse is a reference to Brooke's sonnet, *The Dead* (i), which opens "Blow out you bugles over the rich dead!" and goes on to imply how honourable it is to die for one's country and that, in doing so, a sense of goodness will be returned to the earth. Thomas turns this on its head, by pointing out that no one cares - not even the bugles and that all he does is make "words" (or presumably swears) at the bugles as they call and wake him in the morning.

One senses, unusually for Edward Thomas, an air of irony and humour, but which also borders on irritation here, that Brooke has glorified war and death and also that the army adds pomp and ceremony to everyday events, such as getting out of bed. As an older man (Thomas was thirty-eight when he wrote this), such things may have seemed a bit unnecessary.

This is probably one of Thomas's simplest poems to understand, although the connections with Brooke's sonnets make it more interesting. However, Thomas furthers the parody by making his poem uneven and lacking in harmony, so it is the antithesis of a Brooke sonnet, especially in the final line of each verse, which makes the whole poem clash, but also adds the humour which was deliberately missing from Brooke's poems.

As the team's head-brass

(*Written 27th May 1916*)

The title of this poem, and its first line refer to a team of horses, ploughing a field and the glint created by the sun catching their bridles as they turn back and forth. This team of horses could also be an allusion to the horses at the front, who would have pulled artillery and supply carts through the muddy battlefields.

The narrator notices a couple disappear into the woods in the distance. The first two lines of this poem are symbolic of continuing life: the horses ploughing the field denote the beginning of another year of growth; the lovers going into the woods, presumably for some clandestine affair, demonstrate nature's rebirth. It could be noted, however, that the lovers mentioned are not necessarily people: Edward Thomas often referred to animals and birds as "making love", thus giving them an almost human quality.

The narrator tells us that he is sitting in the branches of an elm tree, which has fallen across the furrows in a section of the field that has already been ploughed. This fallen tree could be a reference to the fallen soldiers in France, who lie in barren fields, just like this one being ploughed. From here he watches the remainder of the ploughing. Charlock is a weed of the mustard family with bright yellow flowers: therefore the field appears to be turning from yellow to brown as it is ploughed, just as the plants, trees and flowers in France have been destroyed. The choice of yellow as a colour provides an internal rhyme pattern with the words "fallen" and "fallow" from the previous two lines.

Each time the horses approach him, as they plough monotonously up and down the field, the narrator fears that he will be run-down, but the ploughman pauses sufficiently each time to exchange a few words, before turning the horses and working his way back up the field. It is as though, by sitting on the dead tree, the narrator (and the reader) fear that he has some affinity with the fallen. Initially the two men talk about the weather, but then their conversation turns towards the war. The ploughman scrapes the blade of his plough as he turns the horses back towards the woods. This also reminds the reader of the blades being used to kill the soldiers at the Front.

The narrator learns that the elm was felled by a heavy snowstorm. This serves as a reminder of the many soldiers who must have died during the cold winters, as though they too have been "felled" by the weather. He asks the ploughman when the tree will be removed and is informed that this will not occur until after the war has finished. Again, there could be said to be a similarity between the tree and the dead soldiers, who will not have proper graves (or in many cases will not have a grave at all) until the war is over. Many dead soldiers were left in No Man's Land and have no known grave, or remained there until the fighting had died down sufficiently for their bodies to be recovered. This conversation between the two men is broken by a gap of ten minutes every time the ploughman turns to plough another length of the field.

The ploughman enquires whether the narrator has served in the war. When he receives a negative answer, he suggests that the man might be avoiding service. The narrator replies that he would happily go if only he knew that he would definitely be coming back. He says that he feels he would not mind losing an arm, but to lose a leg would be a different matter altogether. It is quite likely that Thomas, himself, felt this way - for him the prospect of no longer being able to enjoy his long walks in the countryside would have made life seem intolerable. Death, on the other hand, would be more favourable, since he would no longer want for, or worry about, anything.

The narrator asks whether many men from the surrounding area have gone to the front and died. The ploughman informs him that one of his work-mates had been killed the previous March. In fact, he informs us, the man was killed on the very night of the blizzard which felled the elm tree. This again reiterates the similarity between the fallen tree and the dead soldiers. The ploughman believes that if his mate had not gone to the front and been killed, the tree would by now have been removed. This indicates that, for those not directly affected by death, life carries on much as before.

However, if the tree had been removed, he should not have been able to sit there and have this conversation. In fact, he says, everything would be different without the war. The ploughman believes that, in that case, the world would be a better place. He then decides that, provided everyone could come back alive, everything might be alright. The word "might" is important here since it demonstrates the doubt in the ploughman's mind, that their world will ever be "alright" again.

As the plough turns one last time, the lovers leave the wood, reminding us once more that, for some, life is continuing. The narrator watches the plough work its way through the field. The churning of the mud, once more, brings to mind the muddy battlefields: the uneven tread of the horses and the ploughman call to mind the stumbling and dying soldiers.

This poem continually uses imagery of light and dark: the brass glints in the sunlight; the yellow charlock also represents the sun, light and life which are being cut down by the plough. The woods speak of darkness, since we cannot know what happens in there. The earth also symbolises the dark, in both its colour, its reminiscence of the battlefields and the image of the earth as a grave.

In addition, we are constantly reminded of the images of birth (or life) and death. The very ploughing of the field itself represents the potential birth of new crops, while also bringing about the death of the weeds. The weeds themselves embody plants which serve no purpose - they are deemed useless. This could be equated with the idea that those dying in the war, are being cut down for no reason - their deaths serving no useful purpose. The lovers entering the woods, whether they are human lovers or not, epitomise the suggestion that life goes on as before, and that for some, it will continue to do so, with or without the war.

This poem represents two sides of nature: the death and destruction of war on one side; the continuity of life and the strength of nature itself on the other.

Towards the end of the poem, the ploughman introduces a note of optimism that all might be well; this is short-lived since the narrator feels that everything is being done for the last time. The language used at the end of the poem is down-beat: "crumble", "topple over" and "stumbling", all of which denote finality. *As the Team's Head-Brass* was written while Thomas was trying to decide whether or not to apply for a commission and go overseas to serve, and as such, it reflects his uncertainty about the future.

During his time as a map-reading instructor, he had found himself with less and less time to enjoy his walks in the countryside, which may have led him to reflect on how his life would change should he find himself physically maimed and unable to pursue this activity again. He also worried about the future for his family, should the worst happen. Thomas looked upon his role in the family very traditionally and feared for Helen and his children's security should he not return.

Edward Thomas found it difficult to compare his war-time persona and responsibilities with his peace-time ones and possibly had difficulty contemplating the future in the knowledge that his old world and values would probably have disappeared for ever. Even if he survived, so many others would be dead, that his beloved England, and a way of life he had come to depend upon, might never recover.

This poem bears some comparison with *In Time of the Breaking of Nations* by Thomas Hardy, the point of which is that, from Hardy's perspective, the war would change little; nature would continue to thrive and flourish regardless of the hardships of battle. Thomas, on the other hand, had a different perspective, worrying that the war would change everything. Both poets use similar language, but to very different effect and with different meanings.

The conversational tone of this poem could be compared and contrasted with other poems, such as *Comrades: An Episode* by Robert Nichols, or *They* by Siegfried Sassoon. Both Nichols and Thomas use conversation as a means of telling a story and creating a scene, whereas Sassoon is more likely to use it to demonstrate the personality of someone involved. He also uses speech as a way of reinforcing irony with directly-spoken sarcasm.

Unlike Nichols, however, Thomas's conversation is not between soldiers, but civilians.*Comrades: An Episode* is set in a trench and in No Man's Land, and deals with the relationships between soldiers serving at the front. Conversely, *As the Team's Head-Brass* uses rural England as its location, and deals, fundamentally with the relationship between man and nature. This reflects the poet's concern for his native country by creating a scene which he fears will soon cease to exist.

BLENHEIM ORANGES (GONE, GONE AGAIN)

(Written 3rd September 1916)

This poem was written on 3rd September 1916, while Edward Thomas was resting for a few days, staying at his parents' home at Balham in London, following a training course. By this time, Thomas had almost certainly decided to apply for a commission and overseas posting, which he felt duty-bound to do, rather than remaining safely in England, even though he believed that to go overseas would offer him nothing other than the assured ending of his own life. This pessimism was reflected in much of Thomas's poetry at the time and, over the coming five months he would write only another ten poems, thereby completing his entire collection of 144, all concluded prior to his departure for France. After this, the only pieces of writing which Thomas produced, consisted of letters and diary entries. It would seem that, having made the decision to go overseas, Thomas became retrospective and contemplative of his own role and importance, which is reflected in quite a few of his final poems.

The title of the poem refers to a variety of apple - the "Blenheim Orange" having first been grown near the Blenheim Estate in Oxfordshire in approximately 1740. One might wonder why Thomas chose this particular type of apple rather than, say, a Worcester Pearmain or a Cox's Orange Pippin, both of which have a reasonably long history. However, what they lack is an association with Blenheim Palace itself, which was - and remains - the ancestral home of the Dukes of Marlborough. The first Duke was awarded the estate and his Dukedom in public recognition of having fought (and won) against the French at the Battle of Blenheim (Blindheim) in Bavaria in 1704. Prior to these awards, however, he was better known simply as John Churchill, and was the ancestor of Winston

Churchill, who was born at Blenheim Palace and who, in the early years of the First World War, was First Lord of the Admiralty. This particular apple, therefore, represents English heritage on several levels: not only the aristocracy and political spheres of the Palace and its occupants, but also the country way of life, which has allowed this variety of apple to survive for so many years.

The poem opens with the somewhat depressing and final statement that another summer had "gone, gone again", suggesting that the poet has seen many such seasons pass before. This is not really surprising, given that Thomas was 38 when he wrote this poem, but also allowing for his love of the countryside and nature, by which we may understand that he would have been especially aware of the passing seasons; summer being perhaps the most important of all, as the time for growth and harvest. Thomas describes this season as not particularly "memorable", except for the fact that he has been there to witness its passing - presumably this is noteworthy because so many men are not present any more. However, he qualifies this statement by likening his own presence to that of an "empty quay" which does nothing more than overlook the passing of a flowing river. This statement belittles Thomas's own importance and existence to the point where he would appear - in his own eyes at least - to serve no useful purpose whatsoever. He also creates the impression here that he believes that time, and possibly life, are passing him by, because he is not serving an active purpose, but is merely an onlooker. This shows us how Thomas viewed his role in the war, prior to taking his commission: he felt that his position in England did not amount to doing enough.

Thomas then brings the poem up to the moment, rather than dwelling still in his own thoughts, by describing how the apples are falling from the trees, in the "harvest rain", as though nature is taking care of the harvesting herself. They are not picked by hand, as they normally would be, because the men who would have done this work are no longer here: they are either away fighting or have died already. The impact of the war can, therefore, be seen to affect something as small as an apple, although they will continue to fall from the trees regardless, because they must - rather like the young men themselves, who have fallen in battle - both are inevitable. Thomas reiterates this, recalling that, when he was younger, there were men to do the work, but now they are "lost". The war, he say, has turned such men into "dung". This reference to the corpses of men as nothing more than manure is shocking, but also really quite realistic. Thomas is reminding the reader - harshly - that the dead bodies of this young generation will effectively feed the next generation of crops and trees, nurturing them; that nature will flourish and continue, regardless of the war.

Next, Thomas observes a nearby house, a little old-fashioned perhaps, unloved and uninhabited. Where there should be people and love, there is just overgrown grass, with nothing to show that anybody - with all of their worldly problems - ever lived here. Thomas imagines that in the "beds" of this house, the inhabitants would have felt the "youth, love, age and pain" as they passed through the different stages of their lives between birth and death. He likens himself to the house, which he thinks of as "dead" although he knows that he is, in fact, still alive, which is the difference between them. He is still "interested" in what is happening to him, so his life has not yet become "dark" like the house. In another way, however, he thinks he is similar to the building, in that it has no windows left for "schoolboys" to break with stones, and neither does he. This probably means that he feels as though nothing can hurt or touch him. The eyes are often poetically referred to as the windows of life, so Thomas may be suggesting that his eyes have nothing to fear; they cannot be "broken" because they have already forsaken everything that is of importance to him and, therefore, he has nothing left to lose. So, he may be referring to the fact that, in deciding to go overseas, Thomas was already abandoning everything that mattered to him and felt so assured of his own death that he had nothing else to fear: not even death itself, because he was so well prepared for it.

This is a poem of irregular rhyme patterns, where almost no two of the eight verses share the same metre or rhythm, making this a somewhat jarring poem. However, Thomas was not - especially by this stage - a poet to do something unintentionally, so we may assume that he was trying to induce a feeling of uneasiness and discomfort within the reader, that he could be so accepting of his own fate and his own relative insignificance.

The overall tone here is really of resignation and rather a sense of hopelessness. It is as though, having made his decision to apply for a commission and go overseas, Thomas almost gave up any thought of his own life continuing. When he departed for France in January 1917, he left his wife, Helen, with post-dated cheques to pay the household bills for the next six months, so certain was he that the war would go on and that he would not be returning. This ready acceptance, however, just about manages to avoid tipping over into self-indulgence and self pity (which Thomas fails to avoid elsewhere, such as in his poem *Rain*, for example), and here in *Blenheim Oranges*, he likens his own fate not only to that of the farmers, who have already made their sacrifices to save their beloved land, but also to the abandoned trees and houses that once thrived in a countryside full of life.

The contrast between the imagery of the past, where there would have been apple-picking, harvests, love and youth; and the present, which is dark and bleak, and where there is no-one left, no windows to break, and nothing of significance to give or take away, because nothing matters anymore, is emboldened and enhanced by the unspoken future, for which the young men are fighting and dying. Thomas thought it a worthwhile sacrifice to forsake everything he had to preserve that unspoken, dreamed-of future, and keep it safe for his children, that they might one day walk in those same "footsteps of life", enjoying the beauties of the land for which he and his generation had given their all.

LIGHTS OUT

(Written November 1916)

This poem was written in early November 1916, two months before Edward Thomas went out to France. He had recently been commissioned as a second lieutenant and had been assigned to 244 Siege Battery, Royal Garrison Artillery, based at Lydd in Kent. In early December, Thomas volunteered for overseas service, feeling that this was the only honourable way open for him to serve his country. Nonetheless, this decision was a difficult one, as he always believed that active service would certainly culminate in his own death. The title of this poem refers to the bugle call that is made when the men in camp are required to turn their "lights out" and go to sleep. Thomas wrote, in a letter to his friend and fellow poet, Eleanor Farjeon, that this poem summed up how he felt whenever he heard that call. Although he appears to be literally writing about going off to sleep, this could be taken as a metaphor for death, which at the time, Thomas believed was inevitable.

The poem opens with Thomas's vivid description of how it feels to fall asleep. He equates this sensation with being at the edge of a "deep forest", in which "all must lose their way". This gives the reader the first idea that Thomas's subject may not be just sleep, but also death, since it seems there will be no return from the depths of this forest. The path that each man chooses through the forest, which could be seen as a metaphor for the ending of life, is different, but they all have the same outcome and there is no free will to change this. This observation suggests that all men are equally doomed, that death is inevitable and that, having chosen their course of action, they have abdicated their right to decide what happens to them in the future.

The second verse contains an element of deception, as Thomas suggests that there are different roads and tracks to choose from - and that there always have been - but that these have become blurred, because the men don't really have the same free will and choices as they used to. They must follow the track that leads them to doing their duty, regardless of the personal consequences - and, therefore, this isn't really much of a choice. So, despite having to make a selection about which route to take, either way, they will enter the forest, never to return - in other words, they will "sink". Thomas may be implying that he feels that if he doesn't accept a posting overseas and the inevitability of his own death, he will be forced to live on regarding himself as something of a failure, which means that his options are limited and, either way, he loses.

At this point, Thomas says, upon entering the forest, or accepting death, everything will end: "love", "despair", "ambition", "pleasure and all trouble", no matter whether it was "sweet or bitter", everything will end. This finality is brought about by death - or sleep - that Thomas describes as "sweeter" than even the most honourable of duties. So, he seems to imply that he welcomes death, in the knowledge that he will have fulfilled his righteous task. In verse four, Thomas reiterates this welcoming of death, or sleep, confirming that he gladly turns away from the two things that have always mattered the most to him: writing or literature and those he loves. This sudden remembrance of loved ones, however, seems to awaken a sense of fear, perhaps, as next Thomas comments that he has to go into the "unknown" entirely by himself: he must leave this world behind and enter the dark forest entirely "alone", although he states that he does not "know how". This implies that, although he has made his decision about which path to take and accepted the inevitability of his own death, he has yet to face the actual mechanics of doing it. Thomas, at this stage, had not seen active service at all and had no real experience or comprehension of exactly what might be involved, so this section of the poem might reflect his doubts about his own abilities to face the reality of battle.

The final verse opens with a continuation of this ominous tone, as Thomas describes the forest in terms of its towering height, giving the reader the impression that the poet is powerless and diminutive, when faced with death. This description of the low "foliage" as "cloudy" helps to create an atmosphere which is disheartening and depressing, enhanced by the continued "shelf above shelf" of the canopies of branches, which imply that there is no light, no escape and no hope, once the decision has been made to enter the forest, or once one has accepted death. Although Thomas alludes to the "silence" of the forest, which represents death, he changes the tone here, at the end of the poem: the fear is gone, replaced once again by welcoming acceptance, as Thomas embraces the notion of becoming lost within the confines of death's embrace. Not only does he relish losing his way - as he had guaranteed everyone would do at the beginning of the poem - but he also wishes to lose himself. This implies that Thomas has become unhappy with his earthly life and welcomes the prospect and the relief of escape.

This is a poem which seems fairly typical and symptomatic of someone with depression, although Thomas himself was not, altogether, happy with it, commenting to Eleanor Farjeon "I wonder is it nearly as good as it might be". This remark, however, is also indicative of a depressive mood, demonstrating self-doubt and the need for reassurance. Thomas's mood at the time of writing may explain some of his ready acceptance of death and willingness to embrace losing himself, because he felt dissatisfied with what he was doing, both poetically and in terms of the war, and wondered whether it was adequate. In such a mood as this, a person like Thomas, who was so prone to bouts of depression, might well write of death as an acceptable - even preferable - alternative to life. It would avoid the difficulties and antagonisms which Thomas would have associated with his perceived failings, and may well have seemed like a peaceful alternative to life at that time - like sleep.

Some may feel that the forest is representative of the army - or the war in general: its tall branches representing the power and might of the armed forces and the battles they fight. This can work to a certain extent, as Thomas was about to take the decision to enter into the realms of an overseas posting and, therefore, embrace the comradeship which came with that level of service. Where this hypothesis falls down, however, is in Thomas's descriptions of his willingness to become "lost" within the forest. It seems unlikely that a character such as his would have welcomed this sensation of losing oneself to the army and the war, whereas death (when seen from the perspective of a long and peaceful sleep) may have seemed much more enticing than the ongoing trouble and antagonism of life as it had become.

This poem has a regular rhyme pattern and rhythm, which is fairly unusual for Edward Thomas and suggests that he wanted to allow the reader to focus on the meaning of his words, rather than create a jarring, more uncomfortable poem, where the reader would find the words themselves more difficult to concentrate on. This implies that this poem is one of significance to the poet; that its message of finality and acceptance were vital to him and that he wanted others to understand this. He may not have realised that, for many others, especially those he loved, his seeming acceptance of death was difficult to comprehend. However, Thomas felt - quite rightly as it transpired - that once overseas, his death was inevitable and, presumably, didn't want others to think he was worried or afraid, but that he was prepared for the consequences of his decision.

As with many of his poems, Edward Thomas here only sees the issue at hand from his own perspective, so the fact that he is ready and accepting of his fate seems reasonable to him: he fails, nonetheless, to allow that his friends and family might not find it possible to feel the same.

FURTHER READING RECOMMENDATIONS FOR STUDENTS

Students are often expected to demonstrate a sound knowledge of the texts which they are studying and also to enhance this knowledge with extensive reading of other books within this genre. I have provided on the following pages a list of books, poetry, plays and non-fiction which, in my opinion, provide a good basic understanding of this topic. In addition, a small review of each book has been provided to help students choose which of the following are most suitable for them.

NOVELS

STRANGE MEETING by Susan Hill

Strange Meeting is a beautiful and moving book. It is the story of two young men, who meet in the worst circumstances, yet manage to overcome their surroundings and form a deep and lasting friendship. They are opposites: John Hilliard is quiet and reserved, while David Barton is outgoing and friendly. Despite their differences, their friendship blossoms, as the world around them disintegrates into self-destruction. Susan Hill writes so evocatively that the reader is automatically drawn into the lives of these men: the sights, sounds and even smells which they witness are brought to life. This is a book about war and its effects; it is also a story of love, both conventional and 'forbidden'; of human relationships of every variety. This is a tale told during the worst of times, about the best of men and is, quite simply, one of the best novels ever written about the First World War.

A VERY LONG ENGAGEMENT by Sebastien Japrisot

A story of enduring love, truth and determination. Refusing to believe that her fiancé can possibly have left her forever, Mathilde decides to search for Manech whom she has been told is missing, presumed dead. She learns from a first-hand witness, that he may not have died, so she sets out on a voyage of discovery - learning not just about his fate, but also a great deal about herself and human nature. Mathilde herself has to overcome her own personal fears and hardships and, out of sheer persistence and a refusal to accept the obvious, she eventually discovers the truth. Although this novel does not form part of the main syllabus reading list, it does make an interesting and fairly easy read and is useful from the perspective that it gives a French woman's viewpoint of the war.

REGENERATION by Pat Barker (A-Level only)

This book is, as its title implies, a novel about the rebuilding of men following extreme trauma. Billy Prior is a young working-class officer - a 'temporary gentleman' - who finds himself at Craiglockhart Military Hospital in Edinburgh, having been damaged by his experiences on the Western Front. It is the job of Dr W. H. R. Rivers, to 'mend' Prior, and others like him, ready for them to return to the fighting, while wrestling with his own conscience at the same time. Interweaved into this central plot is the meeting, also at Craiglockhart, of poets Siegfried Sassoon and Wilfred Owen, who are both there to receive treatment. This mixture of fact and fiction within a novel has created some controversy, but it is a common feature within this genre and one which Pat Barker handles better than most. This is an immensely useful book - even if not read as part of the Trilogy - as it takes place away from the front lines, showing the reader the deep and long-lasting effects of battle upon men, whose lives would never be the same again. Due to some adult content, we recommend this book for A-Level students only.

THE RETURN OF THE SOLDIER by Rebecca West

Written in 1918, by an author who had lived through the conflict, this home-front novel gives a useful insight into the trauma of war and society's reaction, as seen through the eyes of three women. Chris Baldry, an officer and husband of Kitty, returns home mid-way through the war, suffering from shell-shock and amnesia. He believes that that he is still in a relationship with Margaret Allington

- his first love from fifteen years earlier. Kitty, Margaret and Chris's cousin, Jenny, must decide whether to leave Chris in his make-believe world, safe from the war; or whether to 'cure' him and risk his future welfare once he returns to being a soldier. A useful novel from many perspectives in that it was written right at the end of the war, and it gives a female, home-front view of the effects of the war on individuals and families.

ALL QUIET ON THE WESTERN FRONT by Erich Maria Remarque

Written from first-hand experience of life in the trenches, this novel is the moving account of the lives of a group of young German soldiers during the First World War. Remarque had been in the trenches during the later stages of the war and this poignant account of war is a must-read for all those who show an interest in this subject. His descriptions of trench-life and battles are second-to-none and his portrayal of the close friendships forged between the men make this an immensely valuable piece of literature. The fact that this, often shocking, story is told from a German perspective also demonstrates the universal horrors of the war and the sympathy between men of both sides for others enduring the same hardships as themselves.

A LONG LONG WAY by Sebastian Barry (A-Level only)

Sebastian Barry's novel tells the a story of Willie Dunne, a young Irish volunteer serving in the trenches of the Western Front. Willie must not only contend with the horrors of the war, but also his own confused feelings regarding the Easter uprising of 1916, and his father's disapproval. Willie's feelings and doubts lead to great upheavals in his life, including personal losses and betrayals by those whom he had believed he could trust. This is an interesting novel about loyalty, war and love, although it does suffer from a degree of historical inaccuracy. In our opinion, due to the adult content of this novel, it is suitable only for A-Level students.

NOT SO QUIET... by Helen Zenna Smith

This novel describes the lives of women working very close to the front line on the Western Front during the First World War, as ambulance drivers. Theirs is a dangerous job, in harsh conditions, with little or no respite. Helen (or Smithy, as she is called by her friends), eventually breaks down under the pressure of the work and returns, briefly, to England. An excellent novel for studying the female perspective, as well as the home front.

POETRY

It is recommended that students read from a wide variety of poets, including female writers. The following anthologies provide good resources for students.

POEMS OF THE FIRST WORLD WAR -
NEVER SUCH INNOCENCE
Edited by Martin Stephen

Probably one of the finest anthologies of First World War poetry currently available. Martin Stephen has collected together some of the best known works by some of the most famous and well-read poets and mixed these with more obscure verses, including many by women and those on the home-front, together with some popular songs both from home and from the front. These have been interspersed with excellent notes which give the reader sufficient information without being too weighty. At the back of the book, there are short biographical notes on many of the poets. This is a fine anthology, suitable both for those who are starting out with their studies, and for the more experienced reader.

LADS: LOVE POETRY OF THE TRENCHES by Martin Taylor

Featuring many lesser-known poets and poems, this anthology approaches the First World War from a different perspective: love. A valuable introduction discusses the emotions of men who, perhaps for the first time, were discovering their own capacity to love their fellow man. This is not an anthology of purely homo-erotic poems, but also features verses by those who had found affection and deep, lasting friendship in the trenches of the First World War.

SCARS UPON MY HEART
Selected by Catherine Reilly

First published in 1981, this anthology is invaluable as it features a collection of poems written exclusively by women on the subject of the First World War.

Some of the better known female poets are featured here, such as Vera Brittain and Jessie Pope, but there are also many more writers who are less famous. In addition there are some poets whose work is featured, who are not now renowned for their poetry, but for their works in other areas of literature. Many of the poets included here have minor biographical details featured at the end of the anthology. This book has become the 'standard' for those wishing to study the female contribution to this genre.

UP THE LINE TO DEATH
Edited by Brian Gardner

This anthology, described by its editor Brian Gardner as a 'book about war', is probably, and deservedly, one of the most widely read in this genre. The famous and not-so-famous sit happily together within in these pages of carefully selected poetry. Arranged thematically, these poems provide a poet's-eye-view of the progression of the war, from the initial euphoria and nationalistic pride of John Freeman's 'Happy is England Now' to Sassoon's plea that we should 'never forget'. Useful biographical details and introductions complete this book, which is almost certainly the most useful and important of all the First World War poetry anthologies.

NON-FICTION

UNDERTONES OF WAR by Edmund Blunden

Edmund Blunden's memoir of his experiences in the First World War is a moving, enlightening and occasionally humorous book, demonstrating above all the intense feelings of respect and comradeship which Blunden found in the trenches.

MEMOIRS OF AN INFANTRY OFFICER by Siegfried Sassoon

Following on from *Memoirs of a Fox-hunting Man*, this book is an autobiographical account of Sassoon's life during the First World War. Sassoon has changed the names of the characters and George Sherston (Sassoon) is not a poet. Sassoon became one of the war's most famous poets and this prose account of his war provides useful background information.
(For a list of the fictional characters and their factual counterparts, see Appendix II of *Siegfried Sassoon* by John Stuart Roberts.)

THE GREAT WAR GENERALS ON THE WESTERN FRONT 1914-1918 by Robin Neillands

Like many others before and since, the cover of this book claims that it will dismiss the old myth that the troops who served in the First World War were badly served by their senior officers. Unlike most of the other books, however, this one is balanced and thought-provoking. Of particular interest within this book is the final chapter which provides an assessment of the main protagonists and their role in the conflict.

THE WESTERN FRONT by Richard Holmes

This is one of many history books about the First World War. Dealing specifically with the Western Front, Richard Holmes looks at the creation of the trench warfare system, supplying men and munitions, major battles and living on the front line..

LETTERS FROM A LOST GENERATION (FIRST WORLD WAR LETTERS OF VERA BRITTAIN AND FOUR FRIENDS) Edited by Alan Bishop and Mark Bostridge

A remarkable insight into the changes which the First World War caused to a particular set of individuals. In this instance, Vera Brittain lost four important people in her life (two close friends, her fiancé and her brother). The agony this evoked is demonstrated through letters sent between these five characters, which went on to form the basis of Vera Brittain's autobiography *Testament of Youth*.

1914-1918: VOICES AND IMAGES OF THE GREAT WAR by Lyn MacDonald

One of the most useful 'unofficial' history books available to those studying the First World War. This book tells the story of the soldiers who fought the war through their letters, diary extracts, newspaper reports, poetry and eye-witness accounts. As with all of Lyn MacDonald's excellent books, *Voices and Images of the Great War* tells its story through the words of the people who were there. The author gives just the right amount of background information of a political and historical nature to keep the reader interested and informed, while leaving the centre-stage to those who really matter... the men themselves.

BIBLIOGRAPHY

The Childhood of Edward Thomas by Edward Thomas

In Pursuit of Spring by Edward Thomas

Edward Thomas - The Last Four Years by Eleanor Farjeon

Now All Roads Lead to France (The Last Years of Edward Thomas) by Matthew Hollis

Edward Thomas - The Annotated Collected Poems edited by Edna Longley

Violets from Oversea by Tonie and Valmai Holt

Minds at War - The Poetry and Experience of the First World War, Edited by David Roberts

Anthem for Doomed Youth by Jon Stallworthy

The Collected Poems of Edward Thomas, Edited by R George Thomas

OTHER TITLES

GREAT WAR LITERATURE STUDY GUIDE E-BOOKS:

NOVELS & PLAYS

All Quiet on the Western Front
Birdsong
Journey's End (A-Level or GCSE)
Regeneration
The Eye in the Door
The Ghost Road
A Long Long Way
The First Casualty
Strange Meeting
The Return of the Soldier
The Accrington Pals
Not About Heroes
Oh What a Lovely War

POET BIOGRAPHIES AND POETRY ANALYSIS:

Herbert Asquith
Harold Begbie
John Peale Bishop
Edmund Blunden
Vera Brittain
Rupert Brooke
Thomas Burke
May Wedderburn Cannan
Margaret Postgate Cole
Alice Corbin
E E Cummings

Nancy Cunard
T S Eliot
Eleanor Farjeon
Gilbert Frankau
Robert Frost
Wilfrid Wilson Gibson
Anna Gordon Keown
Robert Graves
Julian Grenfell
Ivor Gurney
Thomas Hardy
Alan P Herbert
Agnes Grozier Herbertson
W N Hodgson
A E Housman
Geoffrey Anketell Studdert Kennedy
Winifred M Letts
Amy Lowell
E A Mackintosh
John McCrae
Charlotte Mew
Edna St Vincent Millay
Ruth Comfort Mitchell
Harriet Monroe
Edith Nesbit
Robert Nichols
Wilfred Owen
Jessie Pope
Ezra Pound
Florence Ripley Mastin
Isaac Rosenberg
Carl Sandburg
Siegfried Sassoon
Alan Seeger
Charles Hamilton Sorley
Wallace Stevens
Sara Teasdale
Edward Wyndham Tennant
Lesbia Thanet
Edward Thomas

Iris Tree
Katharine Tynan Hinkson
Robert Ernest Vernède
Arthur Graeme West

Please note that e-books are only available direct from our Web site at www.greatwarliterature.co.uk and cannot be purchased through bookshops.

Printed in Great Britain
by Amazon.co.uk, Ltd.,
Marston Gate.